MISSIONS IN A TIME OF TESTING

MISSIONS
IN
A TIME OF TESTING

Thought and Practice
in Contemporary Missions

by

R. K. ORCHARD

THE WESTMINSTER PRESS

Philadelphia

LIBRARY OF CONGRESS CATALOG CARD NO. 65–10319

To
A. M. CHIRGWIN
and
to the memory of
WALTER FREYTAG

Mentors, exemplars, companions
in the understanding and
practice of mission

Published by The Westminster Press ®
Philadelphia, Pennsylvania

PRINTED IN THE UNITED STATES OF AMERICA

CONTENTS

"A new testing time for missions has arrived. . . . Tested missions defend nothing else than the right to bring the Gospel to all men. And in defending that right they are aware that it must not be defended by means of power, but by the inherent force of the witness itself."

W. A. VISSER 'T HOOFT
in an address to the meeting in Mexico of the Commission on World Mission & Evangelism of the World Council of Churches, December 1963

PREFACE

SERVICE as a Secretary of the International Missionary Council, now the Commission of World Mission and Evangelism of the World Council of Churches, has involved me both in reflection on the Biblical and theological basis and meaning of the Christian world mission, and in consultation with mission boards and churches about the changes required in the structure and methods of the missionary enterprise to enable it in the circumstances of the contemporary world to be a more effective and faithful instrument of the Christian world mission. After some years of engagement in this process, there came a point at which honesty with myself required that I put together the somewhat unrelated thoughts and convictions which resulted from it, so that I could discover for myself whether they added up to anything with a coherent meaning. Friends with whom I shared the outcome thought it did, and urged publication. This book is the result.

I am very grateful to my colleagues in the I.M.C. (now the C.W.M.E.) for so arranging our common tasks as to give me the necessary freedom to write it. I am particularly grateful to Bishop Lesslie Newbigin and the Revd. Victor Hayward for reading the manuscript and encouraging me to publish it, and for their constructive comments; and also to colleagues in the London office of the C.W.M.E. who have patiently typed a nearly illegible manuscript and dealt with numerous corrections and additions and deletions. I owe a particular debt of gratitude to the Revd. Dr. H. Cunliffe-Jones, Associate Principal of the Northern Congregational College, Manchester, who read a first draft of the manuscript, made detailed comments of a kind which compelled thought as to exactly what I was trying to say, and at the same time gave me great encouragement to proceed, thereby adding further to all that I owe to his friendship over many years.

While the book naturally owes much to day-by-day work, meetings and discussions in the I.M.C. and C.W.M.E., it should be made clear that it is written in a personal and not an official capacity, and that I, and not the C.W.M.E., am responsible for the views expressed.

The manuscript was completed before the meeting of the Commission on World Mission and Evangelism of the World Council of Churches, held at Mexico City in December 1963.* That meeting was concerned with several of the themes discussed in this book. In particular, it emphasized the need for the Christian mission to meet with men in their life "in the world", outside ecclesiastical structures and habits of thought and action, and within the structures, relationships and activities of human societies. One of its Sections was devoted to "The Witness of Christians to men in the secular world" and another to "The Witness of the Congregation in its Neighbourhood". As the first full meeting of the Commission since the integration of the International Missionary Council and the World Council of Churches at New Delhi, it brought together those engaged in mission in their own country and those engaged in mission in countries other than their own, and began to draw some of the implications from the oft-repeated assertion that mission now faces all six continents. The "Message" issued by that meeting concludes as follows:

> We affirm that this (i.e. the missionary task) means crossing frontiers. This is true of the Christian missionary, who

* The records of this meeting will be published in the autumn of 1964 by Edinburgh House Press, under the title *Witness in Six Continents*.

leaves one culture and one nation to go to people of other cultures to proclaim the Gospel of Christ. . . . But there are other frontiers we need to cross: the Christian congregation must recognize that God sends it into the secular world. Christians must take their part in it—in office, factory, school and farm, and in the struggle for peace and a just order in social and racial relationships. In this task they must seek the power of the Holy Spirit to bear witness by word and by life, to the reality of the living God, in whatever ways are open to them.

We therefore affirm that this missionary movement now involves Christians in all six continents and in all lands. It must be the common witness of the whole Church bringing the whole Gospel to the whole world. We do not yet see all the changes this demands: but we go forward in faith. God's purpose still stands: to sum up all things in Christ. In this hope we dedicate ourselves anew to His mission in the spirit of unity and in humble dependence upon our living Lord.

It is with such themes as this indicates (among others) that this book is concerned. It is in no sense an outcome of or a comment upon the Mexico meeting, but it has seemed useful to indicate in the notes some of the points at which the discussion at Mexico touched on these themes. It may be that the book will be of service in the further discussion of the issues which were brought into prominence at Mexico, and perhaps make some contribution to the understanding and effecting of those "changes" which it saw to be demanded if the missionary movement is to be "the common witness of the whole Church bringing the whole Gospel to the whole world".

R.K.O.

Beckenham, Kent
January 1964

INTRODUCTION

THE increasing interaction between theological reflection and missionary endeavour has frequently been remarked on as a hopeful sign for the future of Christian activity in the world. Theologians in the pursuance of their studies in the various theological disciplines are increasingly led by the logic of those studies to speak about the mission of Christians in the world. Those engaged in the missionary enterprise are increasingly led by the experience it encounters and by the decisions which it has to make to reflect on its basis and meaning. There is a growing conversation between the two.

The stimulus and enrichment resulting for both parties may be gladly recognized. Yet thus far the conversation has remained largely an interesting conversation; its effect, for instance, on either the day-by-day activity of missions or on the broad matters of their organization and operation is not, on the surface at least, very apparent. On the other side, there are no very obvious signs of any radical revision of the traditional theological curriculum arising from it.

So far as missions are concerned, one reason for this is that the insights arising from theological study often do not speak obviously and directly to the issue of policy and practice which missions have to handle in their day-by-day activities; nor are the questions raised by those day-by-day activities those to which theological study commonly addresses itself. The resultant gap is in part inevitable. It is inherent in the different kinds of responsibility discharged by the theologians and by those engaged in the work of missions. The answers to questions arising in the conduct of the affairs of missions in concrete instances cannot be read off from the products of theological study as from a slide-rule. They require decisions which must be made in faith within the actual given circumstances of a particular instance. Such decisions cannot be rightly made by the scholastic application of some theological system, and to attempt to make them in that way is bad for both administration and theology, and is not made any better by the use of Greek terms to denote elements in the administrative or organizational scene! Theology may rightly be looked to to supply the broad background of understanding of the Christian faith and its relation to human experience against which administration must be carried on and decisions must be made, and from which their general direction and broad consequences must be scrutinized. It must not be expected to take over the functions of administration and the daily work of carrying on a mission.

While we may thus distinguish the proper responsibility of the theologians and of those engaged in the work of missions, it may still be suggested that the gap between theological reflection and practical decision is wider than it should be. We are inclined to tip our hat to theology, show it the door, and turn, with a sigh of relief or regret according to our interests and temperament, to the correspondence on our desk and the agenda of the next committee meeting. To acknowledge theological truth and yet not allow it to affect the day-by-day conduct of affairs is to acquiesce in a thoroughly debilitating divorce between word and action. On the side of action—in this case the conduct of missionary affairs—it can mean that activities take on a life of their own, independent of effective control, correction and direction by the word which they are intended to express. On the side of the word—in this case the work of theological study—it can mean that theological reflection is carried on without adequate awareness of part of its raw material, events in the contemporary world and the encounter of Christians with them, which is one way in which God compels us to listen afresh to His word in Jesus Christ and to express it for our own day.

It is chiefly to the former aspect of this divorce that this essay is addressed. It is concerned with some of the issues which arise in the conduct of missionary affairs: but it is concerned to examine them in the light of an understanding of the Biblical and theological meaning of mission. It attempts to listen both to the theologians and to those engaged in missionary affairs, and to discern those points at which they could be speaking to each other, and not past each other. The first part states what I believe to be the central affirmations of the Biblical message, and examines some of its implications for the meaning of mission. It does not offer a Biblical theology, nor an examination of specific passages of Scripture which may be thought to say something about mission. If, as I believe, the Christian mission is inherent in the events to which the Bible testifies, then there is need for an attempt to understand what those events, taken as a whole and in the unity of the Biblical testimony, have to say about the meaning of mission. Some such broad and general approach seems to be required in the missionary enterprise to-day.

The second part approaches the subject from the other side, from the present experience of missions. Some of the issues raised in that experience are examined in the light of the conclusions reached in the first part. This examination does not pretend to provide a "theology of mission". It attempts to discern some of the things which may be learned from the main thrust of the Biblical message about the next steps in missionary action. It therefore tries to start from where we are, and, from where we are, to take seriously what we may learn, from listening to the Biblical testimony, about the direction in which we should seek to move. It has been possible to examine only a limited number of the issues which missions face to-day. The aim has been to choose some of those which both the Biblical message and the contemporary situation indicate as most urgently requiring revision in practice. The point of creative action are those points at which *both* the Bible and contemporary events together question us. If we could see the next steps at such points *and take them*, we would begin both to express afresh the meaning of mission in its wholeness and see that meaning more clearly. We shall certainly not do the second until we have done the first.

A word may be added about the terminology employed. I have tried to avoid the use of some of the semi-technical words commonly used in discussing topics of this kind. This is not because of any aversion to a technical vocabulary as such, which, when properly used in its proper place, is an indispensable tool of thought, study and communication. But in the kind of discussion we are here engaged in, semi-technical terms, such as "church", "world", have tended to become verbal counters, worn thin with use. It is possible to play a kind of intellectual game with them, which is made easier because one of the rules is that the player may give to each counter the value he wishes. This I believe to be one of the minor reasons why discussions of topics of this kind so often fail to "catch on" to the conduct of affairs: the verbal counters come to have less and less connection with the concrete realities with which those affairs must deal. Moreover, the thinner they wear, the more uncertain becomes the meaning of these verbal counters. Take, for instance, this term "world". It is frequently quite uncertain whether it means the whole physical universe, or the inhabited earth, or the life of mankind organized in human societies, or those societies regarded as opposed to or in rebellion against God so that "world" is contrasted with, say, the Kingdom of God (cp. the adjective "worldly"). Or again the term "church" seems to be used to denote (among other meanings) the totality of those who profess Christianity (almost as a synonym for "Christians"), or the churches taken together (almost equivalent to "organized Christianity"), or the

14

local congregation, or the people of God (the relation of which to the empirical churches is of course a main topic of debate in faith and order discussions). It is not necessarily obvious in any particular context which of these meanings is intended, or whether some other meaning is in mind. I have tried to avoid such ambiguities, and to substitute a word or phrase which leaves the specific meaning in less doubt.

It is impossible in dealing with our particular subjects to avoid the use of the word "mission", which has become another such verbal counter, ranging in meaning from the total activities of Christians in human societies to the activities undertaken by an organization for foreign mission in a particular place. In an effort to avoid some of the ambiguity, I use "Mission" with a capital to denote the divine Mission in Jesus Christ, "mission" with a small "m" to denote in a general way the activities of Christians in response to their being sent into human societies, and "missions" in the plural to denote the organizations for mission and their activities, with "foreign" or "home" prefixed where this distinction is required.

A word of explanation may also be necessary regarding the expression "the Christ-event". I have thought it necessary to use this somewhat clumsy phrase to denote the complex act of the birth, life, ministry, teaching, death, resurrection and ascension of Jesus Christ—an act which carries with it the preparation for it in the history of Israel and the consequence which followed from it in the history of the Church. Of course, all this is summed up in the name "Jesus Christ", if one gives full weight to both the personal name and the messianic title. But in contemporary usage the name Jesus Christ does not necessarily call to mind the sense of this total, complex event. Where it seems important to underline the totality of the event, its "happenedness" in history (to use von Hügel's word) and its cosmic dimension, the only brief expression that seems available is "the Christ-event".

Much work has been done recently in the field with which this essay deals. Yet apologies are not offered for adding a further contribution to the discussion. In the endeavour to re-state the meaning of mission in the new framework in which the base of missions and their task are both world-wide, and to examine the policies and practices of missions within this new framework in the light of Biblical and theological thought, the more contributions which can be made from different backgrounds, both confessional and cultural, from different experience and from within different parts of the total service of mission, the better. From their diversity they may speak to our still different situations and in so doing contribute to our understanding of the whole.

This present contribution to the total undertaking is offered chiefly to Christians of the West engaged in mission. It has primarily in mind those who carry responsibility for the policy and practice of missions, whether at their centres or in their work in their home countries or abroad. It is hoped, however, that what is here said may not be entirely irrelevant to others of other parts of the world who are engaged in mission.

The risks attendant on an undertaking of this character are obvious and manifold. The activities in which missions are involved are so many and varied that few can be expert in all the subjects which relate to them. The range of Biblical and theological studies is so wide, and the output of material on them so vast, that anyone who is not a professional theologian cannot possibly master it all; and even professional theologians, it seems, are increasingly tempted to take refuge in some specialism. To attempt to write at the point of interaction of these two spheres is, from a scholarly point of view, to be foolhardy in the extreme.

Yet the point of interaction is immensely important. It may be that someone who is neither a theologian nor engaged directly in the work of missions, but has some contact with both spheres, occupies the kind of position which indicates that he should attempt this piece of foolhardiness, and call attention to the relevant issues.

To try to be a bridge—or rather one plank in a bridge—is to ask to be trodden on. If that invitation is accepted, so that more traffic passes across the gap between word and action, this plank will be content to be walked over.

PART I

CHAPTER I

CHRIST OUR LIFE

THE BASIC CONVICTIONS UNDERLYING THIS ESSAY CAN be briefly stated. They are, first, that in Jesus Christ, God the Creator of the universe has delivered mankind from the distortion and bondage in which its life is held, and has offered a new life in accord with His purpose for man and his world; but most of mankind does not know of or rejects that deliverance. Second, that it is God's purpose to gather up and bring to true fulfilment all things in Jesus Christ. Third, that the mission of the Christian is to participate in Christ's Mission, and is made possible only by that participation.

It is not the purpose of this essay to attempt a systematic exposition of the Biblical and theological basis for these convictions: this is not a treatise on systematic theology. Nor is it our purpose to attempt any proof of these convictions; this is not an essay in Christian apologetics. It is addressed to those already committed to Jesus Christ. It is our aim rather to attempt to draw out some consequences from them in regard to the understanding and practice of the Christian mission in the world to-day. But with that restricted purpose in view, some comments are necessary to indicate, on the one hand, their setting in the Biblical message, and on the other, their bearing specifically on the Christian mission.

Let us look then a little more fully at the first conviction, namely that in Jesus Christ God has delivered mankind from the distortion and bondage in which its life is held, and has offered a new life in accord with His purpose for man and his world; but most of mankind does not know of or rejects that deliverance.

A main emphasis in the New Testament is that the deliverance of mankind from its state of bondage, looked for by the people of God in Israel, and needed by mankind as a whole,[1] has taken place in Jesus Christ. From beginning to end the New Testament is shot through with the conviction that "It has happened!"—that God has acted, that His reign has manifestly come upon men, that His word has been spoken in terms of a human life, that His light has shone in darkness, that the new era has been inaugurated. At the same time, the New Testament is convinced that while the decisive Event of God's act in Jesus Christ has happened, its full consequences are not yet apparent. What is given in Jesus Christ is citizenship in the Kingdom of God, not the full manifestation of the Kingdom.[2] God's last word has been spoken and He will not contradict Himself. But the full consequences of that word, at the end of this temporal existence, remain to be heard.[3] The light of God has shone; but the darkness continues for the present.[4] The new era has been inaugurated; but the old era has not yet been done away—the two eras exist together at present.[5] The new creation has begun; but the old creation has not been fully liberated into the new.[6]

Thus although the decisive act has happened, mankind as a whole does not know of it, and continues its life as though it had not happened.[7] And that life is a life of bondage,[8] a bondage which arises from man's rebellion against God and which results in a distortion of his true existence,[9] which if continued leads to destruction. It is a life whose creative possibilities are also possibilities of destruction and which, left to itself, destroys itself.[10]

Those who, receiving the news of the Event that has happened in Jesus Christ, are laid hold of by it, receive the new life and through faith and hope live in the new era.[11] Their response to the Event is a total response of the whole personality, but four aspects of it may be noted. It is a response of personal commitment to Jesus Christ as deliverer of mankind, and lord of the new era. This commitment is an act of the whole person in response to Jesus Christ as a Person; it is not merely intellectual assent to propositions about Him. And it is both mediated and expressed through the community of those who have been laid hold of by the Event which is Jesus Christ. Secondly, it is expressed in the giving of ultimate devotion to God through Jesus Christ in worship, which is both a liturgical act and a direction of living.[12] Thirdly, it is the expression in daily life within this present era of the new life of the new era which is given in Jesus Christ; it is living as colonies of the divine empire.[13] Fourthly, it is the declaration of the Event to those who have not heard of it or have not been laid hold of by it; it is to be enrolled in the embassy of Jesus Christ.[14]

It is with the last of these that we are specially concerned. But it should be noted that all four belong together and together constitute the response to the Event, Jesus Christ. To separate them is necessary for thought and study, but is unavoidably artificial. To separate them in living is to distort them and can destroy the essential wholeness of the response to Jesus Christ—something which not infrequently happens in the life of the churches and of Christians. Together they constitute participation in the life of Jesus Christ, the life of reality, the fullest kind of existence.[15]

Situated thus in two eras at once, living as alien colonists within "the kingdoms of the world", the life of those who are laid hold of by Jesus Christ is not one of ease and relaxation, but of struggle. To be laid hold of by Him is to be committed to conflict with "the powers of darkness". The New Testament expresses this conflict through a variety of images—light and darkness, the kingdoms of the world and the kingdom of Jesus Christ, life and death. It describes the life of response to Jesus Christ in terms such as "wrestling" and "warfare". To note this is not to ignore the fact that it

23

also describes it in terms of "peace". But the peace that is characteristic of this life is not the peace of withdrawal from conflict, but the peace that is given within the conflict.

Without attempting any full description of this struggle, it may be noted that it goes on both in the interior life of persons and in the external world; it is both psychological and social. This is a distinction which we make in our modern categories of thought. The writers of the New Testament would not have made it; for them the interior world of persons and the external world interpenetrated, and no sharp boundary was drawn between them—an outlook on man and his relations to his environment shared by many people in the world to-day. The point is of importance for our understanding of the Christian mission to-day.

It may further be noted that the struggle goes on within the company of those who have responded to Jesus Christ,[16] and within the lives of the individuals who have so responded.[17] The boundary between the present era and the new era runs right down into the lives of persons; no one can claim to be living wholly within the new era.

Two points about this summary of what has happened in the Event of Jesus Christ must be noted as of special significance for our understanding of its implications for the Christian mission.

The first is that God's deliverance of mankind in Jesus Christ has taken place through an *act*. The emphasis in the New Testament is on God's act in Jesus Christ. "God sent his Son . . ."; this in one form or another is its repeated testimony.[18] The verbs by which it speaks of God are characteristically in the active voice and the indicative mood. When it speaks of the result of that act in those who respond to it, it again speaks of them as God's act—He has "translated us from darkness", "begotten us again to a living hope", "made us kings and priests",[19] and so on. This deliverance is not a matter of abstract ideas or the

24

communication of general principles. It is a transforming event, a life communicated through a person. Furthermore, as an act it is an act in history, an Event within the historical order.

This means that for those apprehended by the Event, the historical order is affirmed. The deliverance is not a deliverance out of our historical existence. It is not a mode of escape from change or a way in which the reality or the significance of historical events can be denied.[20] The message of the New Testament is inextricably—and embarrassingly—linked with the contingent and the relative which are the stuff of historical existence. Any attempt to reduce it to universal ideas or general principles inevitably does violence to it, and, if pressed far enough, such violence as to destroy it, and substitute something else for it. On the other hand, since the Event of which it speaks is the Event of the coming into history of someone from outside it, of the happening which brings a new era into this present historical era, history is not made absolute. Its final meaning is not given within itself, but by an Event which involves a breaking into the historical order. Its goal is not found within itself but in that which is both in and beyond it—at its "end", which is more than the last term in a historical sequence; it is the key term from which the whole derives its meaning. Thus any attempt to domesticate the Event within the limits of any system of thought derived solely from an inspection of the historical order does violence to it. To be apprehended by this Event is to be compelled to take the historical order seriously and to be forbidden to accept it as absolute.

The fact that this act is an event in history gives its universality a particular form. As an act of God for the deliverance of mankind it is an act which is universal in its scope and consequence. As an act in history its universality is given through the concrete and particular. Its universality resides not in general ideas or abstract principles, but in an Event which happened at a particular time and

25

place in history, here and not there, at this and not at some other time. Any attempt to universalize it by abstraction destroys the very thing, the Event, which is the ground of its universal scope and consequence.

The second point to be noted is that when the New Testament affirms that God has acted in Jesus Christ, the term "God" is not an empty concept to be given whatever denotation the hearer wishes. This is no blank cheque on a celestial bank, in which the recipient can fill in the name of whatever divine payer he thinks able to meet the drawing on his account. The God of whom the New Testament speaks is the very definite God who is already known by His acts in history. When the New Testament says "God", it means the God of Abraham, Isaac and Jacob, the God known to Israel through His dealings with them in their history, the God who because of those dealings with His people is known to them as the Creator, and the God who is experienced as still active in history—in short, the God of whom the Old Testament speaks. This is the basic reason why the New Testament cannot be understood apart from the Old Testament.

The Event of Jesus Christ is an act of the Triune God. It is God, the creator and sustainer of all things, who sent His Son into the world. This act is an act in a world which lies in the hand of God the Creator; it is not an act in a world which is unrelated to God or lies outside His control. It is the *same* God who is creator and deliverer, not two gods. It is the same God by whose word the world was made who speaks in Jesus Christ. Deliverance is not out of the created world, nor in spite of the created world, but along with the created world. It is deliverance not from the natural order, but from rebellion against God's purpose and from the consequences of that rebellion. It is characteristic of the Bible to speak of mankind as rebellious—and therefore still related to God against whom it has rebelled; it does not speak of mankind as an unrelated order of beings with whom God has nothing to do except in so far as He may take some from amongst them through His act in Jesus Christ to share the fellowship of His life. The life of response to Jesus Christ is lived in a created and historical world which has not passed outside God's control or finally escaped from His purpose. It is a life lived in accordance with His hidden purpose for all things, made plain in Jesus Christ.[21]

The Event "Jesus Christ" is God's action. The Jesus Christ of whom the New Testament speaks is "the image of the invisible God"[22]—His word "enfleshed", His love embodied, His life poured out. This is the culmination of the New Testament's understanding of what happened in Jesus Christ, and in it lies the coherence and meaning of the Bible as a whole.

But the *recognition* of this meaning in the Event of Jesus Christ is also God's action. To human eyes Jesus Christ remains still only a figure in history—the carpenter's son whose brothers and sisters we know, whom we can firmly confine within the limits of the historical and the contingent. Only those whose insight God Himself enlightens can discern in the carpenter's son the Son of God, can see the King within the incognito, can discern the final within the contingent. The confession that Jesus is "the Christ, the Son of the living God" is not the work of humanity left to itself, of "flesh and blood", but of God, the Holy Spirit.[23]

The Event, Jesus Christ, is thus the act of the Triune God, the deed of God the Creator, God the Son, God the Holy Spirit, one God. It speaks therefore of the constitution of the created world, of the meaning and purpose of the historical order, and of the relation of the inner life of man to both. It brings together the environment in which men live, human existence within it, and human reflection upon it, and sets all under the sovereign and merciful and continuing action of God.

Those who are laid hold of by God's act in Jesus Christ are thereby made heralds of nothing less than this.

CHAPTER 2

MISSION: PARTICIPATION IN GOD'S ACT

IN THE ACT OF GOD IN JESUS CHRIST, MISSION IS IN-herent. It is not simply something deduced from it as a consequence resulting from it: it belongs to the very nature of the act.

This, as has often been pointed out, is apparent in the form in which the New Testament most commonly describes that act: "God sent his Son." It needs to be noted also, however, that that is implicit in the act of the triune God. God the Father sent His Son: God the Son identifies Himself with those to whom He was sent, "being found in fashion as a man".[1] God the Holy Spirit by His action within men provides the possibility of and means for their response to the act of God in Jesus Christ. The act of God is essentially an act of sending forth, of going forth, of penetration. It is, so to say, a missionary outreach into a rebellious world.

It is of the nature of an event in history that it must be reported. Scientific discoveries may be made by an inspection of phenomena and may be arrived at independently by workers in different parts of the world. Ideas may be evolved by reflection on human life and the world of nature, and similar ideas may occur to men in different eras and countries. But an event, if it is to be known, must be reported. If I am to know that William the Conqueror conquered England in 1066, someone must tell me. If I am to know that Jesus Christ was born in Palestine in the first century, was crucified under the governorship of Pontius Pilate, and three days afterwards rose from the dead, someone must tell me.

To experience an event which is of great importance to the one who experiences it is to be moved with a desire to tell others about it. This is a not unimportant reason why the Christ-event naturally gives rise to the Christian mission. To know of the most decisive event in human history is to be moved to tell it to others. It is important that they too should know of the most decisive thing that has ever happened. But the roots of the Christian mission in the Christ-event go deeper than this.

The act of God in Jesus Christ is not simply one event among others—unique, certainly, since every historic event is unique, but wholly of the same character as other events in history. It is an historic event in that it happened in history, but it goes beyond the nature of other historic events. To them the observer, even if he lives in the time and place in which they happen, remains external: they are something that happens outside him or to him. But in this event the observer is caught, laid hold of, made part of the event. He not only hears about it, he becomes a participant in it. It does not just happen outside him: it happens within his life also.

This is part of the meaning of the New Testament teaching about confessing Christ through the Holy Spirit. This is also one way of understanding what it says about the sacramental character of the Christian life. It is implicit, for instance, in what Paul says about baptism as a dying and rising with Christ,[2] and about the Lord's Supper as participation in the body and blood of Christ.[3]

To be laid hold on by Jesus Christ in the way indicated earlier (see pp. 22–25), is therefore to become part of an Event the very nature of which is mission. It is to participate in an act which is a missionary act. Mission is more than a response to what God has done: it is participation in God's act in Christ which is Mission. It is impossible to be grasped by that act without being involved in its missionary character.

To avoid a possible misunderstanding, let it be added

that it is not said that Mission is the *only* characteristic of this act of God in Christ: it is, for instance, also an act of worship and an act of service.[4] Participation in it finds its expression not only in mission, but also in worship and service. The point made here is that this act *is* missionary in character, not that it is *only* missionary in character. This caveat is perhaps worth entering, inasmuch as some expositions of the basis of mission seem to suggest that the *sole* consequence of God's act in Jesus Christ is to make those who respond to it into sharers in the Mission, as though this exhausted the full meaning of the Christian life.

It is very important, therefore, constantly to understand mission as Christ's before it is ours. It is only by participation in Christ's Mission that our missionary activities are kept Christian. It is this which must determine their character, and it is by this that they must ever be corrected and renewed. It is not a matter of affirming that God sent His Son—therefore (and thereafter) we go out in mission: it is a matter of constantly renewed participation "in Christ" in God's act of sending.

This means that all our activities in mission, as well as all our formulations of the meaning of mission, are under the judgment of God's act in Christ. The Gospel is not an ideology, which we can appropriate and proclaim as our own. It always transcends and judges every act of proclaiming it and every human testimony to it. Certainly Christianity as an empirical religion is always in danger of becoming an ideology, and if missions are regarded as or become simply the "propagation of Christianity"— whether Christianity here means a set of propositions or an ethical system or a fixed pattern of worship—then they cut themselves off from their real root and lose the possibility of renewal and real creativity. Only as they recognize their calling to submit themselves to the judgment of God in Christ and so constantly to be renewed in their participation in His act of mission can they be protected from becoming merely propagators of a human ideology.

At the same time, this means that mission is mission in God's world, in the world of which He is both Creator and Redeemer. God's act in Christ must not be divorced from His act in creation: it is the fulfilment of it and therefore makes plain its meaning and purpose. Its redemptive consequences extend to the whole created order: they are not to be confined to an interior, psychological or "spiritual" realm. Jesus Christ is both my saviour and the saviour of the world; neither of these affirmations can be made without the other.

Participation in the Mission of Christ therefore includes participation in His fulfilling of the purpose of the creation. It is being sent with Him into a world which is God's world by right of creation and by right of redemption. And "world" here means both the physical, "natural" world and the exterior, public life of mankind. The purpose of mission therefore cannot be to be concerned only with men's interior, psychological life apart from the life they live as physical beings in the "natural" order, nor apart from the life they live in the exterior world in the "public" realm of human existence—the life that goes on in human societies. Nor can its purpose be to be concerned only with the physical and exterior dimensions of human existence apart from the interior life of persons and their personal acts of mind and emotion and will. It must be concerned with both.

To hold them both together in thought about mission or in the practice of missions is very difficult, especially in an age when our thinking has become so habituated to a false dichotomy between "spiritual" and "material" as to be almost imprisoned within it. It might almost be possible to write a history of missions to show how their practice has been determined by emphasizing either the outward or the interior consequences of God's act in Christ, and how again and again an over-emphasis on one or the other has led to a corrective from the other side. No theoretical

31

exposition of mission, however balanced and acute, will ensure that we draw the full consequences for man's existence in the world of God's act in sending Jesus Christ. Our obedience to that Event in its total meaning is fulfilled only in a practice of mission which constantly subjects its acts as well as its thoughts to the judgment and renewal of the God who acted in Christ and who is still and always active in the physical universe and in human societies, as well as in the corporate and individual lives of His people.

The fact that the origin of mission is in God's act in Christ means that mission is to tell those who do not know the name of *their* Redeemer, the name of Him through whom they are set free into the life of the new age. This is not the same thing as saying that mission is to tell men the name of *our* Redeemer. To express it in the latter way is to run the risk of making the mission ours instead of Christ's; of making Jesus Christ our possession instead of offering ourselves to be His possession; of making primary our apprehension of Him rather than His apprehension of us.[5] To follow that path is to reduce Jesus Christ to the status of a super-psychiatrist, and to end in an intolerable dualism between the interior life and the public life of men, and between God as Redeemer and God as Creator. Mission is to tell men the name of Him who has redeemed them *and* their world.

Three implications of this for the nature of mission may here be indicated. First, it matters that men know the name of their Redeemer. Without that knowledge they remain in the bondage which is the consequence of human rebellion against God's will and purpose. The possibility of entry into the freedom of the sons of God has been opened for all men equally in Jesus Christ: but without the knowledge of who is their Redeemer men cannot use that possibility: they remain in prison.

It matters that men know His *name*. To suppose that one is set free by the knowledge of another name is to remain in bondage to an ideology. It is *this* name, that denotes this specific person in history, which is given in God's act whereby men are set free. The conviction that there is "none other name under heaven given amongst men whereby we must be saved"[6] follows inescapably from the conviction that God has acted in history through a particular person to set mankind free from the consequences of its rebellion. It is part of the historical particularity of the Gospel. To reject it, for instance from the entirely mistaken notion that it implies some kind of arrogance or intolerance on the part of those who speak this name, or from habits of thought that see truth only in terms of abstract universals, is to reject the message of the Bible and the testimony of the Christian churches. Of course, anyone is free to do this if he is so convinced: but he ought to recognize what it is he is doing.

It matters that men know that this name is the name of *their* Redeemer, that in hearing this name they are hearing the name, not of someone who has done something for other people in which they are now invited to share, but of someone who has done something *for them*—fully as much for them as for anyone else. It is this which makes the communication of the Gospel possible, that it is the news of an act which God has done equally for all men. This does not call in question the finality of this name: on the contrary, it is when a name is appropriated as our private possession that it is relative and without finality, for it is then tied to our particular milieu and culture, or even to our own private understanding and formulation of it. We must not be so anxious to safeguard the finality of the name that we confine it to our particular articulations of it in different eras and cultures, and so make its communication impossible. Neither must we be so concerned with its communication that we suggest that somehow this particular name, with all the offence of historical particularity that goes with it, does not finally matter. Or, to put it another way, this name is not discoverable; it must

33

be told, and its telling is at the heart of mission; but when it is told, it is recognizable.

But, secondly, this telling to men the name of their Redeemer is not a process merely of enlightenment. It is not merely an educative or a mental process. The acknowledgment of this name as the name of our Redeemer involves a commitment and a new allegiance which sets us against the forces which are in power in this rebellious human society—pride, self-centredness and supposed self-sufficiency, and the consequences of these which have become embodied and transmitted in human social institutions and in the depths of our personalities. Deliverance from their sway over us involves us in struggle against them. It involves more than a mental or passive recognition of the authority of the Redeemer; it involves a struggle against the powers within us and in our societies which do not obey his authority, and against the results of that disobedience in the realm of nature. The forms of this struggle vary according to the particular sphere of human activity in which they are carried on. It is a continued struggle; it is not one which is concluded in some crisis of conversion. Nor does it go on only outside the bounds of the people of God; it is a continual struggle also within those bounds, against control by the powers of this present age and for obedience to the authority of Christ. To recognize this prevents the misunderstanding of mission as merely a verbal or intellectual process—a matter of the acceptance of propositions about God and His acts. It excludes also any conception of mission which pictures its task as capable of completion in any given part of time and space. Participation in the mission of Jesus Christ involves a continuing struggle against "the principalities and powers", against the forces within ourselves and our societies which claim absolute allegiance from men and usurp the place of God's gracious purpose in every age and in every milieu, as well as a continuing struggle for obedience to Him in the life of any particular church at any particular time. It is a struggle in which the decisive battle has been fought and won at Calvary and at the empty tomb, but which continues until the consequences of that victory are established by the bringing of all things into subjection to Jesus Christ.

Thirdly, the elements in mission here implied must be held together if mission is not to be distorted. Mission involves telling, because there has been an act, the news of which must be communicated, in a particular person, whose name must be told. There can be no mission without "telling"; but telling does not exhaust the meaning of mission. Mission is witness, because the act at the heart of it is not our act. We bear testimony to something that has been done. There can be no mission without the testimony of those who are ready to be cross-examined about the Jesus Christ whose name they tell; but testimony is not the whole of mission. Mission is struggle, because the powers of darkness are real, and those who are set free by God's act in Jesus Christ are thereby committed to struggle against their sway. But struggle is not the whole of mission.

Each of these elements involves the others. To tell in mission is not merely to speak from outside a person or a situation and be content with such external proclamation, like the broadcasting of a recorded advertising slogan to a passing crowd. It is personal communication which involves a struggle to make plain and to achieve understanding, and in that very fact it is an act of witness. Telling involves struggle and witness. It is not the teller's message which is the decisive and final thing—he is telling of something outside and beyond himself, he is bearing witness; but a witness is required to tell of what he knows, and is required to do so with integrity, which involves him in struggle with the forces within himself which would distort his witness and with those outside himself which would seek to make him deny his witness—a struggle which in some circumstances may cost him his physical life; a witness may be also a martyr. And to struggle against the

35

principalities and powers includes telling in whose name we struggle, and in the act of struggling, bearing witness to the power by which we struggle. All three are involved in participation in the Mission of Christ and none can be omitted from our understanding and practice of mission without distorting it.

CHAPTER 3

SOLIDARITY AND SEPARATION

THE AFFIRMATION OF THE BIBLE IS THAT THE ACTS OF creation and redemption are the acts of one God, not of two, and that He alone is God. The alternatives to this, we may note, are an ultimate dualism, in which the god of redemption struggles against the god of creation, or the polytheism of the Baalim, in which every human cultural grouping has its own god of redemption, so that reality can have no final single meaning. To affirm that there is but one God and that it is this one God who acts in creation and redemption is to be committed to solidarity with mankind, since mankind has one Creator and Redeemer.[1]

Missions sometimes seem to have forgotten this consequence. They have sometimes been so conscious of being sent *to* men that they have at least given the appearance of being separate *from* them, cut off from their concerns and separated from their ordinary humanity, eschewing the links of ordinary human intercourse. This has been true of home missions as well as foreign missions. The mission station in a foreign land which sometimes was a place where the ordinary give-and-take of human association was difficult and rare, had its counterpart in the last century in the mission in a poor area of a town where the better educated and better off Christian self-consciously tried to do his duty to the "submerged tenth", but which was often not notable for natural human relationships.

This kind of isolation from one's fellow men to whom one is sent in mission has, of course, a variety of roots. It can spring from a misunderstanding of the nature of mission:

37

"We have a message which you do not have: therefore we are superior to you." It can spring from a fear of contamination by the powers of this age, which implies a mistrust of Christ's power to sustain His own people in the world's life and so leads to the wrong kind of separation. It can be simply a reflection of social and cultural barriers, which means that at this point the powers of this present age are in control of the people of God. It can be, and in most cases probably has been, a combination of all of these.

There is now a trend towards enthusiastic rejection of all such isolationism. It, too, springs from a variety of causes, some of them a correction of the misunderstanding of mission as being from the superior to the inferior, and some of them a reflection of the political and social changes of our time, some of which make any social stratification or unwillingness to mix with those of different cultural backgrounds extremely unpopular. The current catchword to describe the Christian's relation with his fellow men is "solidarity".

Like most reactions, this can be both a healthy corrective and a perilous temptation. It can correct the wrong sort of exclusiveness in mission by recalling us to the realization that God's act in Christ is not our possession but God's gift to mankind, which we receive as part of mankind and not in isolation from our fellows. It can put some necessary critical questions to the contemporary practice of missions. But if uncritically followed it could lead to an equal but opposite distortion of the meaning of God's act in Christ.

For there is also in this act a separation from the kingdom of evil, a rejection of the authority of the powers in the depths of our personalities and in the institutions of society, which deny God's purpose, and which perpetuate and spread an infection of evil through the corporate and the interior life of men. The Mission of Jesus Christ did not only involve "being found in fashion as a man"; it also involved being "obedient unto death, even the death of the cross"—the point of rejection by mankind. The way to the life of the age to come is through a crucifixion, and that implies a rejection both of and by the rebellious elements in the life of this present age. Solidarity by itself is no more the right relationship with the life of this present age than was isolation from it.

Some whose rightful concern is to bridge the gulf between the churches and the daily life of men sometimes seem to suggest that by identifying ourselves with our fellow men in their hopes and needs and sorrows, by entering into the "estrangement" of contemporary man, we shall thereby discover Jesus Christ. This is a dangerously misleading way of stating the matter. It is true that we shall not discover or live with Jesus Christ without entering into a genuine relationship with our fellows in their needs and sorrows. The philosophy of "I'm all right, Jack," in whatever sphere it appears—religious, social, economic or political—is the antithesis of the Christian Gospel. But to suggest that by identifying ourselves with our fellow men we shall discover Jesus Christ is just plainly false. It ignores the fact that Jesus Christ did not only identify Himself with men's hopes and needs and sorrows: He dealt with them in both judgment and mercy. And in dealing with them He not only was at one with men in the Incarnation but also separate from them in the ultimate separation of the Crucifixion.

So those who participate in the Event of Jesus Christ are called both to solidarity with their fellow men and separation from them—and both the solidarity and the separation are "in Christ". We are one with our fellow men because we have been created with them by the same God and because we have been redeemed with them (and not apart from them) by the same God. We are separate from them by the act of response to this particular act of God in history, so that our final allegiance is to someone who comes *into* our humanity from outside it, into this historical order

39

from beyond history, and so separates us from those whose present allegiance is to the "principalities and powers" of this present age.

But this solidarity and separation are held together "in Christ". Jesus Christ dined with "publicans and sinners": He was also alone on the Cross. These two things are not in contradiction: they are the two sides of the inauguration of a new humanity, a new humanity which will not recognize the separations, the classifications of men that arise from human sinfulness, but by the same token will not recognize a final authority in human institutions inevitably corrupted by human rebelliousness, but only the final authority of God, and which knows that a new humanity can only be begun in an obedience to Him that goes to the end in death and a risen life. This is a separation which does not negate the solidarity. It is not the separation of the mystic seeking escape, "the flight of the alone to the alone", the quest for private perfection. On the contrary, this separation reveals the true ground for solidarity in the obedience which inaugurates the new humanity in a risen life, in the life of the age to come; this is not the affirmation of our present humanity, but its re-creation. Men are one in their creation, and in their rebellion: but it is in the life of the crucified and risen Christ that the meaning of that oneness in creation is revealed and the oneness destroyed by rebellion is restored.[2] The Kingdom of God both stands over against rebellious human society, and is its true goal and the ground of its true unity.

It is for this reason that the Christian mission, in so far as it is participation in Christ's Mission, helps to keep open to men the possibility of being really human. In its proclamation of and witness to Jesus Christ, it is witnessing to the true nature of man. And this it does just in so far as it shares in both Christ's solidarity with men and His separation from them. For it is thereby affirming both the ultimate worth of persons and denying that that worth can be truly realized in anything other than obedience to God. It is confronting men with the true meaning of their existence as persons.[3]

The preservation of our humanity (meaning our "human-ness", not "mankind") against the forces which would destroy it or reduce it to something less than human is something which God does for men in two ways. The first is His providential ordering and sustaining of nature and His hidden restraint upon the destructiveness which arises from our rebelliousness. It is this which makes possible man's use of the natural world for the development of his personal life, the increasing freedom from bondage to the forces of nature by his control over it, which is only possible because this is a universe whose order is maintained. It is this also which makes possible the development of human societies in which the extension of orderly process has maintained the freedom of individual persons; for instance, both in the economic sphere in the differentiation of functions, and in social organization through the check on destructive individualism by the extension of the rule of law. It is this also which has prevented man's rebelliousness from destroying him, because the consequences of his rebellion are held in check by God's providential control of events. In all this activity God is "hidden", in the sense that it takes place whether or not men recognize its source in Him. In His preservation of the natural world and in His restraint of the destructiveness of human rebellion, God expresses His concern for men as persons. Men may respond to that concern in their handling of the affairs of daily life, even though they do not know or do not acknowledge its origin in Him.[4]

But, second, God is active through those who consciously acknowledge and accept His rule in Jesus Christ. Through them the boundaries of our humanity are extended and fuller possibilities of realizing truly personal existence are made plain. Thus, for example, the ordering of human societies by the extension of the realm of law has provided a framework within which some kind of personal existence is possible, whereas it is not possible in a merely anarchic existence. But the care for persons as persons irrespective of their place in or worth to society has sprung from those who consciously accepted the rule of Jesus Christ; for instance, in the care of the destitute, the defenceless, the slave, the social outcaste.

This concern for persons has passed into the thinking and acting of men and communities, and many who have struggled sacrificially for the personal existence of their fellows have owed no conscious allegiance to Jesus Christ or, indeed, have expressly repudiated such allegiance. But it is from the acknowledgment of Jesus Christ as Lord and Saviour that this concern for persons must constantly be renewed. For man's personal existence is constantly being threatened in new ways. Technological advance gives man increasing control over nature and so increases the range of his possible freedom: it also brings the risks of depersonalization in a "mass society" and of concentrations of power which can erode the areas of personal freedom. Those who acknowledge the goal of history to be in the new Man Jesus Christ should be the first to see both the possibilities and the risks, and should be in the forefront of the struggle so to use the possibilities of the technological era as to defend and extend the boundaries of personal existence.

Or again, human economic and social institutions can extend the sphere of personal existence by their differentiation of function and by providing for that variety of activity which is possible in a diversified society in which the rule of law is acknowledged. But all such institutions can also become threats to personal existence, partly by the rigidity which overtakes all human institutions, so that what began as an extension of personal living ends by becoming a restriction of it, and partly by their infection by human pride, which makes of them ends in themselves and claims for them ultimate allegiance. The one leads to the ossification of societies, the other to economic or political totalitarianism. Both are threats to personal existence. Those who acknowledge Jesus Christ as alone having the right to ultimate allegiance should be the first to see the threat of any claim to absoluteness on the part of any human institution, and should be in the forefront of the struggle to secure the recognition that all human institutions are relative, and so to re-establish the sphere of personal existence over against any claim to absoluteness.[5]

Participation in the struggle for personal existence is involved in participation in Christ's Mission. For in the end it is a question of what god men worship. The golden calf, Nebuchadnezzar's golden image, the unknown god of the Athenians all have their counterparts in the contemporary world; for instance, in the acceptance in practice of the ultimacy of economic goods, in the claim for absolute allegiance to a state or nation, in the refusal to be committed which is the practical agnosticism of many to-day. The struggle for personal existence within the framework of an ordered society is at bottom the struggle for the possibility of the worship of God in Christ: the proclamation of Jesus Christ is the ground from which all struggle for personal existence derives its meaning, purpose and incentive. These two are the obverse and reverse side of the same coin, Jesus Christ, True God and True Man.

But mission is not a quest for human welfare. Its objective is not to establish or safeguard living room for personal existence. That is a consequence of mission, not its primary purpose. Missions in practice have not infrequently regarded it as the latter, and from time to time have based much of their appeal on and directed much of their activity towards the increase of the possibility of personal existence amongst those whose lives have been restricted by oppression or poverty. Mission, however, does not arise from any distinction between "bond" and "free" in the political sense nor between "rich" and "poor" in the economic sense, whether these distinctions are between

43

nations or within one nation. Nor does it depend on any category of human "need" if "need" means "need within this historical order". It depends simply on the distinction between those who know the name of their Redeemer and those who do not.

This is far from saying that Christians are not concerned with the deliverance of captives and the relief of poverty and the meeting of human needs in this historical order. They are necessarily and deeply concerned with such things, because love of one's neighbour is a command and a consequence that are integral to the claim of God in Christ upon them. To love one's neighbour is an inescapable obligation on Christians, and it has to be worked out in terms of social justice as well as in terms of personal service. That obligation and the obligation to tell of and bear witness to the Christ-event are both inescapable, and neither is a substitute for the other.

Nor can they be finally separated from each other. The Christian life is a whole. In the life of the individual Christian and in the life of the local congregation such obligations as these must be fulfilled together, however advisable it may be for organizational purposes to distinguish them on other levels of Christian activity. But if it is our purpose to think about the Christian mission as such, then to distinguish it in thought from the meeting of human need in this historical order seems not only legitimate but necessary.

For mission as such is concerned with the ultimate in life. It is concerned with the final issues with which men are confronted in Jesus Christ. Because it is participation in the Mission of Christ, it must inevitably raise with men the "boundary questions", the ultimate issues of final meaning and ultimate allegiance. It is concerned with the short term and the contingent only as the form in which such "boundary questions" meet us in our historical existence and as the opportunities and occasions for the expression of obedience to the ultimate and final which confronts us in Jesus Christ. It is saying to men: "The end of the ages has come upon you—here and now. The ultimate meaning of human existence, its final goal, real and full life are here and now set before you." Mission is participation in the Event which stands on the boundary between the life of this age and the life of the age to come: it cannot be content to raise less than life-and-death issues.

At the same time it has to raise the ultimate questions within this historical order. For the Event in which it participates is a particular historical event. Mission is therefore concerned with the ultimate *in history*, not in abstraction from history. So mission cannot escape from the conditions of our historical existence. It cannot, for example, escape geography: mission is always mission in some particular place in space, amidst all the contingent factors of environment and culture and language which are thereby involved. Any attempt to escape from these actualities inevitably destroys the character of mission, substituting the declaration of abstract principles for witness to Jesus Christ, and a communication to men's minds for the sharing of a life with the whole man. Similarly, mission cannot escape from its setting in time. It is urgent that men know the name of their Redeemer because the end of the ages has come upon them, the Kingdom of God is at hand, and it is not given to us to know the times and the seasons, so no man can tell how long in this historical order may be left for the decision to accept and enter or to reject and refuse to enter. (Incidentally, we may note that the real urgency of mission lies here, and not in any expected changes of political systems or social patterns which are often adduced as reasons for urgent action: such reasons are not consonant with the understanding of history which is given to us as we listen to God's word through the Bible.)

The calling to mission must therefore always be answered in concrete situations. It must always be answered within the historical order, and the response is therefore fragmentary and specific, not generalized. In terms of corporate decisions, by a church or a mission board for instance, the response is in terms of acceptance of responsibility to bear witness to this Event in this and this particular place at this particular moment in time. In terms of the individual Christian, the response is: "I am called at this time to witness to the Event in this particular place." (The choice of place may well be, of course, not a private choice, but a choice made by a responsible board or committee: but its acceptance is a specific response in a concrete situation.) The current slogans such as: "All Christians are missionaries" are dangerous half-truths; they obscure the concreteness of the specific response required by participation in the Event which carries all the particularity of an event in history.

To be content with an abstract and generalized response is to retreat from history. It is to try to escape from the actualities of the historical order in which God has set us and within which He looks for our response to Jesus Christ. This means that we are not masters of the destiny of missions. What happens to them or through them (except within very narrow limits) is not within our control. They may in fact be used of God to articulate His purpose in history within particular places at particular times. When we look back over the course of history, we can sometimes see that this has been so and note traces of the way in which God has used missions in the fulfilment of His total purpose for a people. But it is not given to missions to determine the course of history, or even to discern beyond doubt and in detail the ways in which God is carrying out His purpose in any given set of historical circumstances in to-day or to-morrow. This does not mean that missions do not take into account historical circumstances and trends in determining their courses of action. But it does mean that they are not the controllers of God's purpose in history: they are its servants, and they serve that purpose by their witness to the Christ-event. What

46

follows from that witness, in terms of the process of history, is in God's hands, not theirs. What they are sure of is the end; and it is to the end that is in Jesus Christ that they testify.

CHAPTER 4

GATHERED INTO THEIR HEAD

THE SECOND CONVICTION ON WHICH THIS ESSAY IS based may be stated in the words of the letter to the Ephesians. God "has made known to us his hidden purpose . . . that the universe, all in heaven and on earth, might be brought into a unity in Christ".[1] This passage sums up the Biblical message of the universality of Jesus Christ—that He is the focus and the goal of God's purpose not only for history, but for the whole universe. To this universality, mission is at once response and testimony.

Two comments need to be made about the universality of God's purpose in Jesus Christ. The first concerns its nature. God's act in Christ has a universal reference because of its concentration in a person and because of its penetration into history through an event. It is not a universality of abstraction, such as may be achieved by stripping off the layers of the particular, the local, the concrete. This is the kind of universality rightly sought in science and achieved in its purest form in mathematics. The proposition that two and two are four achieves its universality by not saying "two what?", and especially by not asking what kind of thing is represented by the "two". It achieves its form of universality by abstraction from the individuality and concreteness of particular things. The universality of God's act in Jesus Christ is precisely not this kind of universality. It is the universality of concreteness, of penetration, which through a particular person and a particular event in history sums up (*anakephalaiosasthai*, Eph. 1: 10) and expresses the total meaning of God's purpose for mankind, as the last act of a play or the final stanza of a poem sums up and expresses the meaning of all that has gone before and gives the whole its coherence and purpose, or as the central figure of a painting brings the whole into shape and balance, where without it the shape and patterns and colours were a formless chaos.

This kind of universality excludes any conception of mission as the mere transmission of abstract propositions. Mission must always be the testimony to *this* person and *this* event in such a way that men are brought to see their relation to it, and to find the meaning of their existence within the pattern that is summed up in Jesus Christ.

The universal reference of this person and this event are not achieved by mere extension. They are universal by right of finality. This is the ultimate point of reference, the final goal of all things: therefore it is universal in the sense that it is to this goal that all things move and by reference to this that the meaning of all things is seen. The universality of this person does not depend on His acceptance by all men; it is His by right of the fact that He is God's last word. Belief in the final authority of Jesus Christ and belief in His universality go together; neither can be held without the other.

This marks off this kind of universality from the forms of universality which are appropriate in the scientific or political spheres. The universality of a scientific proposition depends upon its being infinitely extensible. The emergence anywhere of a new fact which contradicts it compels the substitution of a new hypothesis to take account of this new fact. It would seem to follow that all scientific propositions are inherently provisional, and that their universal reference is bound up with their provisional character. The universality of Jesus Christ is bound up with His finality; it is the universality of the drawing together of everything into Him in whom is every ultimate meaning. Acceptance of this universality is commitment to a person, in terms of the personal meaning of things: it is not the acceptance of a proposition whose universality is dependent on its infinite extensibility.

In the political sphere, universality depends on participation in a common system of law and custom, either freely accepted or imposed by force. The universality of any political régime is bound up with its extension, either by force or consent. Its claim to universality can no longer hold as soon as it encounters a different political system which effectively maintains itself against it. The universality of Jesus Christ is not thus dependent on the extension of His régime, either by force or by consent. It is given in His character as God's last word, as decisive, and it is there, whether or not it is overtly accepted by men. It is in this sense a hidden universality, the reality of which is not openly seen in this historical aeon.[2] It is not therefore capable of coercive proof. Its acceptance is an interior act by a person, not the exterior extension of a system.

The universality of Jesus Christ is thus a universality not of suppression, but of re-creation. It draws all things into God's purpose from within themselves by their re-creation into the true purpose for which they were created. It is the universality of a kingdom of personal consent, by renewal from within resulting in conformity with God's purpose.

If missions are to fulfil the purpose of Mission in being the response and testimony to this universality, they must conform to the nature of this universality. They must not, for example, suppose that it is their function to *make* the Christ-event universal. It is already universal: their function is to bear witness to that. Nor must they suppose that, in order to ensure that the Christ-event is universally acknowledged, it is their function to extend a single ecclesiastical structure throughout the world. This is to confuse a political form of universality, expressed through a historical institution, with the form of Christ's universality. Their witness to the universality of the Christ-event is essentially the witness of commitment and participation,

50

through which they may become the instruments of communication and re-creation.

The second comment about the universality of God's purpose in Jesus Christ is simply to call attention to the fact that it concerns "*all* things". It is concerned with the totality of things: it is not confined to a section of life, to some department labelled "religious" or "spiritual". There is nothing outside the providential governance of God, and that providential governance has its focus and goal in Jesus Christ. No part of this created universe and no area of human activity is finally autonomous. Man's rebellion against God is essentially his assertion of final autonomy over against God, both in himself and in the forms of his human activity. This is the root cause of the disorder in the life of this historical era and of the disintegration from which man suffers, both in his interior being (the conflicts in the human *psyche*) and in his society (in the spheres of economic and political life and in cultural disintegration).

But this created universe, and man within it, remain God's creation even in rebellion. Those who are committed to Jesus Christ know this through Him, through His embodiment of God's hidden rule. Their mission is therefore to bear witness to the hidden rule of God, which has claimed them in Jesus Christ, in *all* things, in every part of human activity. God uses this witness to liberate all things from the bondage resulting from rebellion into their true end in Christ.[3]

Something of this kind is frequently said in discussions of the universality of the Christian mission. What is perhaps less frequently referred to is the significance, for the form and method of the mission, of the measure of freedom and responsibility God has accorded to man.[4] Within His creation God has given men creative powers and limited, but real, freedom to exercise them. In this lies man's responsibility. It is not therefore sufficient to say that no sphere of human activity has final autonomy over against

God. It is also necessary to recognize that the spheres of human creative activity have a rightful though limited autonomy, and to consider how that limited autonomy may be rightly exercised. Rebellion against God does not lie in men's use of their creative gifts: it happens when the claim is made that the products of such use have completeness and finality in entire separation from the giver.

It is essential that Christians recognize the rightful, though limited, autonomy of the spheres in which men exercise their creative gifts—the spheres of economics and politics, of education and the arts, of science and technology.[5] Unless these are recognized as spheres within which God grants to men freedom in the use of creative powers, the behaviour of Christians towards them is likely to fall into one of two opposite errors. We may, on the one side, dismiss or ignore them as of no consequence for the Christian mission, and as a result confine that mission to the interior, psychological sphere of human life. This is to deny the universality of Jesus Christ and to exclude Him from the whole public and corporate area of human living. It is to give to these realms of human creative activity a final and not a limited autonomy, and so in effect to accept the idolatry which accords to the products of human creativity an absolute claim over men's allegiance.

On the other side, we may refuse to recognize the rightful, limited autonomy of such spheres and claim to be able immediately and directly to control them in the name of Christ, without respecting their limited but real freedom, or accepting the necessity to understand and work through the discipline, the ethos which is appropriate to each. It can result in a refusal to welcome the discoveries and insights into the nature of the created world or the possibilities for the development of man's control over nature and for the better ordering of human societies which they can provide. This is, in the first place, to fail to take seriously God's acts in creation. It is to put men's creative gifts outside the purpose of God, and to suggest that the spheres of their use are of no significance in God's purpose in creation. Secondly, it is to try to anticipate the consummation of God's purpose, to seek to live as though this historical aeon had been wound up and all the powers God had given men were now used consciously and willingly in joyful obedience to His purpose, while all that was opposed to His purpose had been done away. We are not given the right thus to try to anticipate the consummation of God's purpose or to abbreviate the era in which men have the possibility of decision to accept or reject God's offer of life in Christ.

This anticipation of the consummation is what medieval Christendom was tempted to attempt, when it sought to impose conformity with the will of God in Christ by the use of ecclesiastical control and supernatural sanctions, expressed through human institutions, over all spheres of human living. It was thereby denying the limited autonomy of politics and economics, education and culture, science and technology which God has accorded to them in this historical era, and asserting the right to control them directly in the name of Christ. This is the wrong way to witness to the final, penetrating, re-creating universality of Christ. It is to seek to use the forms of universality appropriate to science and politics to affirm the universality of Christ to which they are not appropriate. The attempt broke down at the Renaissance and the Reformation by its inherent contradiction. The use of ecclesiastical power in a form appropriate to political power subjected it to the corruption to which political power is subject, and provoked a reaction which asserted political freedom from such ecclesio-political control. And, at a deeper level, the denial of the right to use man's creative gifts in freedom led to a reaction which asserted the freedom of scientific investigation and artistic creation from ecclesiastical control.

The reaction in some spheres asserted not only freedom from ecclesiastical control, but absolute freedom. When a church succumbs to the temptation to assume the prerogative of God, it is not surprising if in reacting against that church, men also react against God. We are to-day confronted with the need to re-affirm the sovereignty of God in ways which will recognize the rightful autonomy of spheres of human creativity and at the same time provide a unity of purpose in human living. This calls for bearing witness to the true goals of life as we know them in Jesus Christ, but without any attempt at ecclesiastical control of the spheres of human creative action and without claiming (within those spheres) supernatural sanctions for the policies advocated. At the same time it calls for witness to the limitation of the autonomy of all such spheres by resistance to any claims that they are absolute.

Such a quest for genuine human freedom and responsibility would seem to be part of the Christian mission in its witness to the universality of Christ. That witness must combine responsible participation in human creativeness with resistance to the idolatry of absolute claims for the products of that creativeness. It cannot fulfil the task either by attempting to re-assert ecclesiastical control of human societies and their varied spheres of activity, or by ignoring them and allowing their pretensions to absoluteness and finality to go unchallenged from within. Its form must be determined by the form of universality of its Lord, by penetration, not abstraction; by re-creation from within, not by suppression. It is under this form that a new conception of Christendom, which testifies to the universality of Jesus Christ in all things, must be sought.

In the Bible, this gathering of all things to their true centre in Jesus Christ is seen as accomplished particularly through the gathering of the "nations" to Him. This is so in the Old Testament prophecies of the "nations" coming to share in the worship of the people of God, and in the New Testament affirmations about men coming from east and west and north and south, and sitting at table in the Kingdom of God,[6] about the breaking down of the wall of

54

partition between Jew and Gentile,[7] and about the nations coming to the new Jerusalem.[8] Whatever be the precise denotation of the words translated "nations", "Gentiles", in any particular passage, the total impression produced by the Biblical evidence is that the accomplishment of the universal purpose of God in Jesus Christ involves the human groupings in which men live. It is effected through man in his social setting, not through man isolated from his social setting. The Christ-event, inaugurating a new humanity, through those who participate in it draws the "nations" into the purpose of God. Those who participate in the Mission of Christ become the hidden focus of the "nations" of which they are members, and so instruments of their re-creation from within.[9]

It is perhaps necessary to note here that the Biblical distinction between "the people of God" and "the nations" (between 'am and goyyim, laos and ethne) puts the people of God in a particular classification. Israel is one nation among others; yet as the people of God it is a nation re-fashioned by God's action at the Exodus and by the bond of a covenant of which He is the initiating party. As the bearer of God's revelation and the instrument of His purpose, Israel is set apart from other nations. With the coming of Jesus Christ within it, this distinctive character of the people of God as a new kind of "nation", a new "race", is made clear and the era of the fulfilment of God's purpose through it is inaugurated. It is thereafter not an earthly city, standing on a hill in Palestine, but "the Jerusalem that is above" which is "free" and "our mother".[10] It is the "people for God's own possession" called out of darkness into light and made into a community in Christ, who are the participants in Christ's Mission in the world ("that you may declare the wonderful deeds of him who called you out of darkness into his marvellous light"),[11] not any of the national groups of the ancient or modern world.

The Biblical testimony thus excludes the identification

of the people of God with any nation. But, by the same token, it also puts a strong question mark against attempts to make religion the cohesive element in any nation. Human creativity at work in the sphere of communal life is always seeking to cement its social structure by some religious adhesive, whether it be the divine Emperor of the Roman Empire, or the identification of the national life with one of Asia's classic religions, or Marxist orthodoxy in a communist régime, or the religion of Yahweh regarded as the defence of Israel as one nation among others, or Judaism as the basis of the life of the State of Israel, or Christianity as the official religion of Western Christendom or of the Western nations which are its "successor states". The Biblical witness is against such attempts to use religion as the integrating element in human societies. Such attempts confuse the "gods of the peoples"—the products of human creativity, who are "idols"—with the Lord who "made the heavens"[12]—the living God who of His own free choice calls men in Christ out of every human grouping and for all of whom God's house is to be a house of prayer.[13] They mistake the products of human creativity within history for the divine Event which comes into history from beyond it. They look for the possibility of the reintegration of our broken humanity within this historical order: but the Biblical testimony is that the new community is created by an act of God into history from outside it, which results in a new kind of community whose basis is beyond the historical order, and whose life transcends that order and cannot therefore be identified with any human grouping.[14] The new humanity in Christ is within the "nations" of this historical aeon: it is not to be identified with any of them, nor regarded as of the same genus as any of them.

This is not to say that the life of a nation lies outside God's purpose, or is a matter of indifference for the fulfilment of that purpose. On the contrary, it is to suggest that men's creative achievements in the realm of government

56

and the ordering of the life of the community have the same kind of relation to His purpose as any other product of human creativity; as, for instance, the realm of the arts, or of scientific investigation and the application of its results to human needs. The nation has the same possibility of being open to God's purpose or resistant to it as these other spheres of human creative activity. It is suggested later (see pp. 134–141), that it is part of the mission of God's people to keep the nation open to God's purpose, a task which is obscured if the distinction between the people of God and a nation in the historical order is blurred or lost.

While the New Testament evidence is scanty and not easy to interpret, it suggests to us that the "nations" are thought of as belonging to this historical aeon, and that at its consummation their function will have been completed. At any rate the conception of men exercising a limited but real autonomy in the sphere of national life through the acts of government and the organization of society is not out of keeping with the picture of the Great Assize in Matthew 25, where the nations are judged according to their treatment of Christ as He is found among the afflicted of His brethren in mankind,[15] or with the vision of the Apocalypse (Revelation 21) of the glory and honour of the nations being brought into the heavenly city; for both of these refer not to this historical aeon but to the end, the consummation of history in God's purpose where indeed "all things", including the products of human creativity so far as they are in accord with His purpose, will be "summed up" in Christ (Eph. 1: 10).

If the foregoing is a right understanding of the Biblical evidence, then it suggests the lines of the task of mission to "the nations". On the one hand, the mission must respect the legitimate autonomy of human groupings. They have their distinctive contribution to bring, within the purpose of God, to the re-created humanity in Christ. The mission is therefore mission to men *within* those human groupings, inviting their obedience to Jesus Christ as the centre of

57

their living from within their "nation", and not seeking to draw them out of their human groupings as though these had no part in God's purpose.[16] On the other hand, the mission within those human groupings is a witness that they are not final or absolute, but are subject to God's final word in Jesus Christ; they find their true meaning only as they are drawn into God's purpose in Christ and so are brought into the line of fulfilment of all things in Him.

Such an approach to the mission to the "nations" requires some comments. It may be objected that "nations" are not the product of human creativity and cannot be rightly regarded as analogous to human creative activities in such spheres as economics or artistic creation. Reflection on what constitutes a nation suggests, however, that this objection is not well-founded. A nation may be said to be constituted by a group of people who share a common history and have the will and the means to act together as a political entity. This is to say that a nation comes into being as a result of human creativity in the sphere of communal life, acting on the given circumstance of the natural world and the events of history. This is not different in principle from human creative activity in the use of materials (economics) or in ordering the life of society (government) or even in the use of shapes and sounds and movement to express meaning (the arts). In all such activities there is a "given" element and the action of human creative powers in its use. The proportion of the two varies according to the nature of the activity: the purposes to which the given element and the creative activity are directed are different. But the process in principle is the same, and its theological status is the same: it is an exercise of human freedom and responsibility, with the possibility of being obedient to God or in rebellion against Him. And it is the presence of the mission, which articulates the Christ-event within the process, that brings that choice into the open and requires a decision.

It is not untrue to the Biblical evidence to see the mission to the nations in the world of to-day as including mission to all human groupings that result from the exercise of man's creative activities. It is obviously illegitimate to equate the modern nation-state with the concepts in the Bible represented by such terms as "nations". In Biblical usage such terms denoted much looser, more general notions of human societies than the term "nation" tends to do in modern usage, vague though that concept is. With the increasing differentiation of function in modern societies, it is legitimate to understand the "mission to the nations" as including mission to men in the variety of their social groupings. In other words, the mission must be not only to men in the relationship they have created in the British or the Indian or Chinese nation, but also in the relationship they have created in, for instance, the various forms of industry, or in the different spheres of scientific research or the technological application of science, or in education or the arts. Whatever view is taken of the exegetical question here raised, a man is what he is at least as much as a result of the fact that he is a farmer or a factory worker or an actor or a teacher, as of the fact that he is British or Indian or Chinese. Unless the mission can speak to him *qua* farmer or factory worker or actor or teacher, a large part of his existence will remain untouched by its message. More than that, unless the mission can be planted in the midst of the human activity, whether farming or factory production or drama or education, in a way similar to that in which it has been planted in the midst of the human activity which produced the British or Indian or Chinese nation, then whole areas of human creative action will continue to succumb to the idolatry of making absolute claims for themselves, for lack of witness within them to the universality of Jesus Christ into whom it is God's purpose to sum up all things.

CHAPTER 5

MISSION IN ALL LIFE

THERE ARE FEW SPHERES IN WHICH THERE IS GREATER uncertainty about the objectives and forms of the Christian mission than the sphere of human creative activity and its expressions in the life of communities. It is in this sphere that many of the theological questions which we find most baffling arise with great sharpness—the relation of nature and grace, of world-history and salvation-history, of community and church. Most of the theological work on such questions in the past has been done in the context of "Christendom", in which the assumption is made that the total community as well as the Church was in some sense consciously seeking to be obedient to God in Christ. This is an untenable assumption in the contemporary world, whether in lands where other religions are dominant or in those where a traditional Christian allegiance is ignored or rejected. Christian responsibility towards the creative activities of men has to be thought through afresh in a context where those activities own no allegiance to God in Christ. This compels re-thinking from fundamentals, and that task has only just been begun. The theological basis for a fresh formulation of the Christian mission in this sphere is only beginning to become available.[1]

Furthermore, the concepts with which thought about human creative activities, and especially about their expression in human societies, has operated in the past have been in general appropriate to static societies. Such terms for instance as law, government, institution, class structure, nation or family tend to suggest a fixed, even a pre-determined and given pattern of function and relationship. At least to one who has no expert knowledge in this sphere, it seems that we need also some fundamental rethinking in the sphere of the sociology of human creativity, if the concepts with which we work are to be appropriate to the highly fluid state of human societies in the contemporary world.

Yet, whatever the difficulties, to ignore this aspect of the responsibility of the mission is to limit Christ's universality and implicitly to deny God's purpose to sum up *all* things in him. Moreover, men are persons in community and not in abstraction from their relationships within communities. The Christ-event must be so told that it lays hold of persons in the whole web of relationships through which their personal existence is expressed. It must be so told that it gives new meaning and direction to their exercise of their creative gifts within those relationships, and does not allow men to suppose that the exercise of those gifts is either irrelevant to or outside the purpose of God in Christ. The use of those gifts must be seen to be a sphere for obedience to Jesus Christ.

On the other side, it can never be the duty of Christians simply to confirm men in their creative activities or to affirm the corporate activities resulting from them. For in men's use of them there is an inherent rebelliousness which distorts their use and imports into them the seeds of self-destructiveness. This distortion and tendency to self-destruction infects the resultant corporate activities and the social structures which express them, and in which they become, so to speak, objectified and take on a life of their own. Man is not only a person in relationships: the kind of person he is, is to a considerable extent determined by the relationships in which he is set: our social structures mould us. Those social structures embody and transmit the consequences of human rebelliousness, as well as the consequences of true creativeness. They therefore constitute an obstacle to obedience to Jesus Christ as well as a sphere within which that obedience is possible. Is not this one reason why men will do things corporately which individually they would reject as unethical?

It follows that Christians' responsibility in their own use of creative gifts cannot be one of simple acceptance or rejection, but must be one of penitence and openness to redemption. They are to be used "under the Cross", which implies rejection as well as acceptance, and transformation as well as affirmation. This we understand in terms of a Christian's own action. But do we understand what it means in terms of those corporate structures of society in which Christians are inevitably involved?

Two forms of action by Christians are, it seems, required in the discharge of their mission. The first concerns their participation in corporate activities in the community; for instance, as citizens, as participants in agriculture or industry, as sharers in cultural activities—education, the arts and so on. The Christian must engage in these activities, not only because he cannot contract out of his society, but because to attempt to do so is to deny that human creativity is a gift from God. In other words, he must be glad to be involved for Christ's sake. On the other hand, he cannot be unreservedly committed in such activities, because he is aware of the element of rebellion and self-assertion over against God which is involved in them. His involvement is always a critical involvement. His decisions within them are made, not indeed without respect for the discipline and ethos which belong to the particular activity and are part of its rightful autonomy, but not solely within that context; they have a constant reference to an event which comes *into* that activity from outside it, the Event of Jesus Christ. From that reference he will discern both positively those tendencies in the activity which he should support and encourage, and negatively those which he must oppose and resist. Such decisions cannot be made either from outside the activity in question or in advance. They must always be made from within it and in the actual moment of decision.

But is this participation and involvement of Christians in the corporate activities of human societies all that is required in the discharge of the Christian mission in this sphere? (It is, of course, assumed that along with it will go the discharge of other Christian duties such as membership in the Church and sharing in its worship, and the corporate and individual acts of service to men which are other necessary responses to the Christ-event.) It seems to us that it is not. The last paragraph attempts to delineate briefly the witness in corporate activities of the individual Christian. But can that witness in this sphere be a full witness unless it is rooted and reinforced by a corporate witness of the Christian community?

The temptation at this point is to say: "Of course a corporate witness is also necessary," and then go on to speak about the Church. Some analysis is, however, needed before that transition can be made. If that "portmanteau" word *Church* is being used to mean the whole company of Christians, then in a sense (though not a very precise one) any corporate action by a group of Christians is action by the Church. (The question would, however, remain of the forms of organization needed for such corporate action for witness in society.) But the word *Church* carries a more specific connotation than this. It commonly connotes a body of Christians organized in a continuing institution with a definite structure. The question is whether the Christian mission in society requires a corporate witness by a church in this sense—by a church as institution.

A simple positive or negative answer to that question would be misleading. In the first place, a church by its very existence in a human society is a witness to Jesus Christ, and so is part of the Christian mission in that society. However much more it is, a church is a sociological entity within a human society, and that society cannot be unaware of its existence, even though it may try to ignore it. Yet in so far as a church is true to its distinctive character, its life is rooted in a commitment beyond the sphere of human creative activity within this historical aeon. Just in so far as it expresses, in its own life and existence as an institution, its creation by Jesus Christ—in the way in which it orders its affairs, in the relationships between its members within it, in its dealings with human society around it—to that extent it will by its existence be a witness to Him within human society. Furthermore, in so far as its life is governed by the Christ-event, it constitutes a sphere within a human society in which the final meaning of all human creative activities is acknowledged to lie beyond themselves, a sphere in which the ultimate reference of human creativity to God the Creator is gladly and freely acknowledged in the act of Christian worship. Its continuing existence as a church is a check on the pretensions to absoluteness and finality of the spheres of human creative activity. (But it will only continue to be so if it recognizes that, as an institution in society, it also is tempted to make such pretensions for itself: and if its own life is genuinely and constantly open to judgment and renewal by Jesus Christ.)

In the second place, however, just because a church is one institution among others in human society, as an institution it cannot penetrate the life of other institutions. It is set alongside them, in some cases (e.g. the state) within them, yet it necessarily remains separate from them. If this were not so, it would lose its identity as an institution. Its members, of course, penetrate and share in the other institutions of society, and, as we have seen, it is essential for the Christian mission that they should do so, and should recognize their life within the various institutions of society to be a sphere for the expression of their Christian commitment. But a church as institution remains distinct from other institutions.

If, thirdly, a church as institution tries to penetrate the institutions of society, it will be in danger of trying to operate in this sphere by the method of ecclesiastical control. When a church acts as an institution, its acts must necessarily have the character of churchly acts. Within its own sphere, it may rightly claim for its acts and judgments its own distinctive authority. If, however, it attempts to act directly *as an institution* within the spheres of other institutions in human society, it can hardly avoid claiming for its acts and judgments within those other spheres the distinctive authority which it rightly claims for them in its own sphere. But to import that distinctive kind of authority into other institutions in human society can be to infringe the proper autonomy which belongs to them, and to expect an acceptance of churchly authority from a society the majority of whose members do not acknowledge the basis on which churchly authority rests. In the institutions of human society, acts and judgments must be assessed on their merits as contributing to the common human life of society; it is difficult for a church acting as an institution within society not to claim for its acts authority on other grounds than this.

What seems, then, to be needed is a means for corporate action by Christians in witness in society which will neither claim the sanction of churchly authority nor commit a church as institution by its judgments and actions.

Such an instrument is needed, first, to help individual Christians in the very difficult decisions that have to be made in the various spheres of corporate activities in society. It does not seem to be very helpful to keep on saying that Christians must bear their witness in society without providing some means whereby we can be helped to reach the concrete decisions which that witness requires. Since those decisions have to be made in actual situations as they arise, some means is needed whereby Christians who have to make them in any given sphere—in a particular industry or profession for instance—can meet with one another to check one another's individual judgments and to assist one another to see those decisions in terms of a common loyalty to Jesus Christ. If such a meeting can be

65

related to some existing church meeting, well and good, provided that it is recognized as not thereby acquiring any kind of church authority for its actions or conclusions.[2]

There is an interesting and encouraging growth of various forms of centres and organizations aimed at providing this kind of opportunity. They are, however, still regarded as somewhat esoteric and for the "top people", and they usually involve Christians only occasionally and for short periods. What is required is an acceptance of the need for this kind of help as a regular part of Christian living, and the provision of it in ways which will be constantly available locally, in the places where people live their daily lives and are involved in making the decisions.

But this is a means of helping individual Christians to bear their witness in their own places in society. The further question, whether any corporate witness in action is required in these spheres is one which is most perplexing. The issue may perhaps be put in this form. The witness of individual Christians to God's purpose to sum up all things in Christ can be made in the corporate structures of human societies only within the limits imposed by the fact that these structures are not consciously and explicitly directed to the service of God in Christ. They are subject to His hidden rule; they are not open to His manifest reign. If Christians are to bear full and open witness to Him as Lord and Saviour, should they provide means for the expression of men's creative gifts in structures which are explicitly and specifically aimed at being expressions of obedience to Jesus Christ, for the sake of manifesting in corporate activities what that obedience means in the particular circumstances of one country and culture and one sphere of activity in society?

The issue is put first in this abstract form because to put it first concretely raises all sorts of other issues which tend to obscure the point here concerning us. Concretely, however, the question presumably is: "Should Christians attempt to provide, say a Christian factory, in order that there may be an explicit corporate witness in the realm of industry to the fact that our creative gifts come from God and that the goal of their use is in Jesus Christ?" It must be kept in mind that the question posed is not, should *a church* run a factory for the sake of this witness, but should *Christians*, i.e. in this case a group of Christians engaged in any event in this particular industry? It must also be kept in mind that this question concerns Christian witness; there may be occasions when, for the sake of serving some human need, it is clearly the duty of Christians, possibly even of a church as such, to run a factory—for instance to provide employment for refugees—but that is another matter and has another purpose in view. It should also be noted that the question does not suggest that the factory be run as an evangelistic agency, so that the test applied to it would be whether or not people were brought to belief in Jesus Christ through its existence: the purpose envisaged is that of manifesting more fully, in terms of the particular industry, the consequences of using powers of creativity in explicit acknowledgment that their goal is in Jesus Christ. It may further be observed that action of this kind is not unknown in Christian history, for instance in the various forms of economic enterprise engaged in by monasteries or other explicitly Christian communities, or by some foreign missions in the modern era, though such instances had other purposes, as well as this one, in view.

It does not, however, appear that corporate action of this kind for this purpose by Christians is theologically justified. In the first place, it would all too easily lead to the assumption that such a "Christian" factory (to continue with that illustration) was somehow immune from the effects of rebelliousness which affect the "non-Christian" factory; so far from being a witness to the summing up of all things in Christ, it would in fact be likely to contribute to the pride of Christians, who are all too prone to forget that their institutions (not to mention themselves!) are involved in the consequence of human rebelliousness.

The factory could not exist in an economic vacuum any more than individual Christians can: it would necessarily be involved in the total economic structure and from that point of view would be no more free to express obedience to Christ than any other factory. It would create the illusion of being a Christian witness while being in fact a temptation to Christian pride.

In the second place, such an approach implies a wrong understanding of Christian responsibility towards the community. It suggests that Christians can bear a witness to Jesus Christ in separation from the community of which they are part—in this instance the economic community. It would thus be an attempt to escape from that solidarity with our fellow men which is one inescapable condition of Christian living.

There may indeed be circumstances arising from external pressures which compel Christians to engage as Christians in corporate activities of this kind. But to engage in them by choice as an act of witness in some sphere of human creativity would seem to be theologically questionable. Between the witness of Christians in those spheres, on the one hand, supported by corporate consultation as indicated and by the worship of God in Christ in the company of His people, and, on the other hand, the existence of the Church as an institution—distinct from the other institutions in society and with its own characteristic loyalty and way of life— there would seem to be no middle course of Christian witness which can be justified on the ground that it is required by participation in Christ's Mission. That negative conclusion has some consequences for the practice of Christian missions about which something will be said at a later point in this essay.

Participation in Christ's Mission requires a relationship of Christians to their sphere of human creative activity which can only be described in paradoxical terms. It is one of involved detachment, of critical responsibility. The Christian cannot contract out from these spheres of the

68

common life, because they are the spheres in which God-given creative powers are to be used, and because he may not deny his solidarity with his fellow men. Neither can he enter them without reserve and uncritically, because they are constantly tempted to make themselves absolutes, and because they do not own a loyalty to Jesus Christ.

Looked at from the point of view of this paradoxical relationship to human societies, the essential form of all mission is "foreign" mission. Every form of Christian mission comes into the sphere of human living in which it works with a centre of loyalty which is outside that sphere. The Christian is inevitably an "alien" in the sense of one whose ultimate allegiance lies elsewhere than in any sphere of human activity or any framework of human relationship.[3] In so far as he participates in Christ's Mission, he must always be putting to human corporate activities questions that arise from outside these activities. Yet he must put these questions not as one who stands outside, but as one who is involved in that sphere of activity. He must press his question to the point of final purpose. Thus the Christian mission in industry, for instance, must find ways of raising the question of the ultimate purpose of industrial processes, and not be content with an answer in terms of cheapening the product or effectiveness in competition with a rival concern. On the other hand, if the Christian raises the question of ultimate purpose from *inside* the industrial process, he cannot do so without taking seriously the economic issues, such as the cheapness of the product and the competitive conditions of the market. From inside the process, merely idealistic assertions about ultimate goals have no effect. The real but limited autonomy of the sphere of human creativity here rightly asserts itself. If the Christian mission has been a nuisance outside the area of traditional "Christendom" because of its "foreign-ness", it must learn to be a similar nuisance within those lands once known as "Christendom", where it is also "foreign", because its ultimate allegiance is outside this historical aeon, and its calling is to confront men with that Event which inaugurated a radically new humanity.

At the same time, like the foreign mission in the geographical sense, it cannot remain outside, uninvolved in these spheres of human activity. "Identification" within them is as necessary as the "identification" of the foreign mission with the people of the foreign country in which it works. This means that the Christian mission in industry or politics or the arts must "know the language" of these spheres; it must be skilled in their ways of thought and action, and able to speak with those engaged in them from within them.

All this suggests that if, by our knowledge through Christ of the creative activity of God, and by our commitment to the universality of Christ, we are required to regard the "nations" of economics, politics, the arts, as spheres of mission, then we need serious and sustained effort to evolve the means for the discharge of that mission appropriate to its purpose. The "foreign" missions, when they began to take seriously the "nations" of the Pacific or Asia or Africa, had to evolve organizations for the discharge of their task, to study the kind of persons required for it, and the training that was suited to it, to learn (and in many cases to reduce to writing) the languages in which they were to work, and to find ways of engaging the support of and keeping informed the general body of Christians. We have no grounds for supposing that the "foreign" mission to the unevangelized continents of economics, politics, the arts, will require any less strenuous thought and effort in organization, training, support, or that it requires any less devotion, skill, and courage in experiment.

To remain responsible towards the corporate activities and structures which express human creativity without being ultimately committed to them: to be genuinely involved without totally accepting—this is a delicate and costly process.

There is no rule of thumb to guide us in it. It calls for positive discrimination in each actual situation, a discrimination which springs from that deeply personal trust in Jesus Christ which Christians call faith and from that continuing concern for persons at the deepest level of their existence which they call love. It is part of the meaning of "living under the Cross" which was the point of deepest involvement with men and the point of final separation from human rebelliousness. To live under the Cross is to be called to say in the given circumstances of a particular country and culture and sphere of human activity both "Yes" and "No" to the results of human creativity, and so to be the bearer of a life from beyond the Cross which is neither the affirmation of human creativity nor its denial, but its true fulfilment in a new life, the life of a risen Lord, in whom all things are made new.

CHAPTER 6

THE MISSION IS CHRIST'S

THE THIRD CONVICTION UNDERLYING THIS ESSAY
is a consequence of the other two. It is that the Mission
is Christ's before it is ours: it is only ours in so far as we are
"in Christ".[1]

In the preceding chapters we have tried to take seriously
the Biblical testimony that both the decisive act in the redemption of mankind and the activity which created and
sustains the universe are God's action. The involvement of
Christians in mission is rooted in their sharing in God's
activity, through their sharing in the life of Christ. In the
very act of commitment to Jesus Christ, of laying hold on
Him who has laid hold on them, they are committed to
witness. That witness is only possible through the crucifixion and rising again from the dead of Him whose life
they share. The crucifixion is the ultimate solidarity with
men in the depths of our human finitude and in the consequences of our rebelliousness: and it is the ultimate separation from men in our assertion of ourselves as self-sufficient
over against God, for it is an act of complete obedience to
God and therefore the manifestation of His final reign.

It is through participation in the crucifixion that we are
enabled to share the solidarity with and the separation
from our fellows which are essential to witness to God's
acts, and to the articulation of them in particular times and
places and in particular forms of human culture and activity. The rising from the dead is the manifestation both of
the universality of God's reign and of its victory over the
consequences of human rebellion. It is the assurance that

in Christ we can be raised above the limitations of our human finitude, that in Him we are not finally bound within this historical aeon or imprisoned in particular times and places and cultures, and that in him the forces of rebellion are defeated and the "principalities and powers" are subdued. It makes possible a universal mission, because it is the victory over finitude and rebellion. (It may here be noted that in the New Testament the universal Mission of Christ begins *after* His resurrection.)[2] And the crucifixion and the rising from the dead are part of one act: the glorification is in the crucifixion, as the Fourth Gospel testifies.

The Christian mission is thus to make articulate, explicit, open, God's acts as He has declared them to us in Jesus Christ, including His activity in creation. Its consequence is both to confront men explicitly in specific circumstances with the decisions which we are required to make before God, and to open to them the possibility of liberation from the consequences of our rebellion against God. It is to affirm both God's reign and the offer of participation through Christ in that reign.

This is not to say that the reign of God is present only where the mission is, or to confine His Kingdom to those times and places where it becomes articulate through mission. That would be to make God subject to His witnesses, and to testify not to the Lord of all, but to a tribal Baal. To say that God's Kingdom is only present where it is borne witness to is to be in danger of that idolatry which puts the Church, or the Bible, or the mission, or the missionary or minister in place of God; an idolatry which we all repudiate in principle, but which has a strange power of asserting itself in practice. God's reign is over all, and is not dependent on human testimony to it.

That is something of which we need constantly to be reminded, especially those of us whose calling is to be wholly occupied with ecclesiastical and missionary affairs. At the same time, we are not allowed to draw from it the con-

73

clusion that the human testimony to God's reign as made known in Christ and to the offer of participation in it through Him is a matter of indifference, or even a kind of impertinence towards God and our fellow men. Thus to regard it would be to reject the Incarnation, to try to be wiser than God, who has chosen to act in a particular person at a particular point in history and to speak His word within and in the terms of our historical existence. It would be to refuse to participate in the Mission of Christ— to refuse to speak again that same Word within the particularities of our own time and place and circumstances, to reject participation in Christ's life.

To acknowledge both God's self-subsistent reign and His manifestation of it in Jesus Christ is to acknowledge that the Mission is Christ's before it is ours and ours only in so far as we are "in Christ". To draw the consequences from this for our understanding and practice of mission in the actual circumstances of our time is an exacting task. It calls for a mental and emotional liberation from bondage to our inherited institutions and modes of thought, which are subject to the inescapable tendency to assert human rights over our institutions and our mental constructs and so make them our own empires and means of our own self-assertion. None of us alone has attained such liberation, and as we seek it together we need to do so in the penitence which does not take refuge in the false humility of drawing back when our Lord comes to us with towel and basin, but is ready to let Him wash our feet.

That having been said, it seems necessary, with such humility as He may grant to us, to try to indicate a few of the consequences of the affirmation that the Mission is Christ's before it is ours. In so doing we recognize that our understanding of those consequences cannot fully escape from the prideful elements of the institutions and forms of thought in which we have been nurtured, and so needs both correction and completion by others whose inheritance is different.

74

In the first place, some consequences follow for our understanding of the Church. Here we are using that word to denote those corporate, historic bodies which as corporate institutions have the intention of confessing Christ and living by His life. (This is intended to denote the sense in which we are using the word, not as an ecclesiological definition.) Whatever else may be said of such bodies, either within them or from outside them, they are the places where the intention which underlies their existence and in which their members at any given time share to a greater or less extent, is to worship and glorify God in Christ. They are the places where the intention is consciously, willingly and explicitly to accept and confess the reign of God as He has manifested it in Jesus Christ.

Now one consequence of affirming that the Mission is Christ's before it is ours is to prevent our identifying the churches with the Kingdom of God. It is even to prevent our identifying the Church, if that word is used with any reference to a visible institution within this temporal era, with the Kingdom. To make that identification is to make Christ the prisoner of His witnesses. It is to claim that the Mission is ours, not ours only in so far as we are "in Christ". The churches trust the promise of Christ to be present with His people: they cannot *guarantee* His presence. He is Lord over them, not subject to them. They are witnesses to Him, not proprietors of Him.

It is God the Holy Spirit who takes those acts of worship, witness and confession which the churches offer to Him and makes them signs of the Kingdom and tokens of the life of the age to come. It is in the Holy Spirit that the churches share in the life of Christ, and it is He, and not they, who finally determines what of their life is truly within the sphere of God's reign in Christ. This does not absolve the churches from the responsibility of constantly seeking to make their life a sphere in which God's reign is openly present, by their honouring of the testimony of the Bible, by their faithfulness in the use of the means of grace,

75

by their searching for obedience in their common life both within themselves and in their activity in the communities in which they are set. But it does mean that when they have done all they can in faithful obedience, the decision of what in their life is the manifestation of the life of Christ is God's decision, not theirs. They also stand under His judgment and live by His mercy. Only in so far as they acknowledge that they thus live from God and not from themselves can they be saved from becoming instruments of human self-assertion and be made witnesses to Him who came to give His life. The churches' real life is a constantly renewed life, and one condition of that renewal is the recognition that they are not guarantors of God's presence but that all their activity is at God's disposal.

Yet in His mercy God does use the life of the churches thus offered to Him as witness to His acts in Jesus Christ. However deformed by human self-assertion or weakened by human faithlessness the churches become, God honours whatever offering of their life to Him, whatever faith in Jesus Christ there may be within them and uses these to call the churches to new life. It is this possibility of renewal from within that most distinguishes the churches from other human historic corporate institutions. It is therefore questionable whether it is within the competence of men to pass the judgment that such and such a church is dead, so long at least as there remain within it any who own themselves as belonging to Jesus Christ.

The very existence of a corporate body bearing His name is itself a witness to Him, and to that extent both a reminder amongst men that they are subject to Him and an offer to them of the possibility of sharing His life. Beyond that minimal witness, the effectiveness of a church's witness will depend on the extent to which the ordering of its life on the one hand, and its involvement with the community in which it is set on the other, keep it open to the life which its Lord offers it. To seek to particularize the conditions of such openness would require a full discussion of ecclesiology and of the churches' responsibility to the community. Here we can do no more than point to the fact that such openness requires again that separation from and solidarity with men that is the fruit of sharing in Christ's Mission.

A second and analogous series of consequences wait to be drawn in the sphere of missions. By the word *missions* here we mean those organizations specifically devoted to the proclamation of the Christian Gospel, whether in their own or in other countries. All such organizations are meant, not only those in the West. For our immediate purpose, it is irrelevant whether such organizations are committees or boards of a church or associations of individual Christians. (Again we may observe that this is no formal definition, but merely an indication of the sense in which we are here using the word.)

Missions in this sense are human attempts to point to God's acts in Jesus Christ. They are not to be identified either in theory or practice with Christ's Mission. They rely upon Christ's promise to use such human testimony to bring men to know him; but they cannot guarantee that it is Christ who is actually proclaimed, or that in so far as He is, men will recognize Him for what He is. They are witnesses to the Gospel, not proprietors of it; they are sharers in Christ's Mission, not lords over it. Their relation to it is one of faith.

This means that no mission can guarantee that it is "The Mission", whether by the purity of its doctrine or the devotion of its workers or the visible results of its work. It is God the Holy Spirit who in His mercy may use the human testimony of missions to bear witness to His reign in Christ and to bring men to commitment to Christ. But this is His decision, not the mission's.

This does not absolve a mission from the responsibility of seeking constantly that its witness may be a faithful witness, by honouring the testimony of the Bible both in the methods of its work, by the careful choice and training of

77

its workers, by seeking obedience to Christ in the ordering of its affairs both internally and in its involvement in the life of communities, and by keeping itself livingly related to the whole company of those who confess Christ as Lord. But it does mean that when it has done all it can in faithfulness and obedience, the decision as to what in its activity becomes part of Christ's Mission belongs to God and not to the mission.

To equate missions with Christ's Mission is fatal. Just because they are concerned with the proclamation of the ultimate and the final, they are peculiarly susceptible to the temptation to become instruments of human self-assertion, whether the "self" be an individual, or a group holding a particular doctrinal position, or a particular nation or culture or "way of life". Just because they rightly concentrate on specific tasks, the proclamation of the Gospel in certain particular places, it is easy for that specific task to fill their horizon to the exclusion of others, so that they come to regard their existence and work as in some sense giving them a superiority over other activities. Just because they are involved in witness to the universality of Jesus Christ, it is easy for them to succumb to delusions of grandeur as though the Mission depended on them. The defence against such distortions is the constant recognition that the Mission is Christ's before it is theirs, that Christ's Mission is not coterminous with theirs, and that if He uses their service for the furtherance of His Mission, that is a consequence not of their orthodoxy or devotion or efficiency, but of His graciousness.

And yet, God in His mercy does use the activity of missions, presented to Him, to witness to His reign and to offer to men the possibility of participation in it. Despite their corruption by human self-assertion, despite the narrowness of the views some of them have held about God's purposes, despite even the divisiveness of which they have often been guilty (if in the contemplation of that saddening spectacle we may take comfort from Paul's word about

Christ being proclaimed even through divisions), Jesus Christ has been proclaimed. It is part of the mystery of the divine grace that despite all their human sinfulness, despite all their mixed motives, God has used the service of groups of men and women to make Jesus Christ known amongst all peoples, and has so used what was worthy in their marred and spoiled offering of service that amidst almost all the world's peoples there are those who are committed to Him.

Since we have here discussed churches and missions separately, it may be well to note that missions cannot in principle be separated from churches. A church is in principle the people drawn into the Christ-event and thereby committed to sharing in Christ's Mission. There can therefore be no final dichotomy in principle between church and mission. But the relationship between the two is not one of simple identification, for mission is not simply a function of a church; it is a gift of Christ to a church. This matter and its organizational consequences are referred to at a later point in this essay (see p. 152 ff.). Here it is sufficient to note the necessity of an intimate relationship between missions and churches.

A church is not the Kingdom and missions are not the Mission. Each is corrupted if it makes that identification. But a church is the sign of the Kingdom and missions are instruments of the Mission. To despair of them is to deny what God has done in them and through them. The Mission is Christ's; but after we have acknowledged that, we may know that He calls us to share in it, and may see in these all too human organs of activity means which God deigns to use for the fulfilment of His purpose.

CHAPTER 7

MISSION AS WITNESS

SINCE THE MISSION IS CHRIST'S BEFORE IT IS OURS, AT the heart of mission is witness. Mission is essentially the act of pointing to Jesus Christ. It is testimony to something done. It is to point away from oneself—whether the "self" is an individual or a group or an institution or a way of life —to Jesus Christ. Yet it is an act of involving the self, for in the end witness involves commitment; the witness must be prepared to be cross-examined, and should not expect the process of cross-examination to be always controlled by judges' rules. In principle, he must be prepared to stake his life on the truth of that to which he testifies. This is so even when the cross-examination does not extend to physical martyrdom. Essential though verbal testimony is, it can never be effective except as the testimony of the life is congruous with the testimony of the words. It has been said that the only way of validating the Christian faith is to bear witness to it in life.[1] This is true also of the testimony of corporate bodies as well as of individuals, of churches in the varied levels of their life, in the local congregation, the national and international organization, of missionary organizations in the varied forms of their activities and structures. They must expect the cross-examination to extend beyond their words to the nature and methods of their organizations and to their activities and the quality of corporate life which they display within themselves and in their relation with the communities in which they live, including the corporate structures of those communities. And they must expect the standard applied in that cross-examination to be, not necessarily the standard commonly accepted by the community, but the standard to which they themselves point in their words, the life that is in Jesus Christ.

Since their business in mission is to point away from themselves to Jesus Christ, and since in doing so they themselves cannot escape cross-examination, it is essential that the nature of their organizational structure and the quality of their corporate life should be such as to direct the attention of those who cross-examine them towards Jesus Christ. From the standpoint of Mission, this is the essential test of all church orders, of all Christian organizations for community service, and of all organizations concerned with mission, whether in the home country or abroad. It is a searching one.

Witness of such a character involves a distinctive relationship both to Jesus Christ and to the persons to whom witness is borne. It is only possible for those whose primary purpose is participation in the Mission of Jesus Christ. It is impossible for those whose purpose is to proclaim Jesus Christ for the sake of securing some other objective. It is possible precisely to the extent that the purpose of participation in the Mission of Jesus Christ becomes the dominant purpose in the intention and action of the witness. (This has something to say to the place of the nurture of life in Christ amongst those engaged in mission and to the means and discipline provided for that nurture in the programme of missions.) At the same time it implies a distinctive relationship to those to whom witness is borne. It is a relationship in which the desires of the witness are subordinate to the needs of the persons to whom he seeks to bear witness, a relation of subordination, almost of servitude. The horizon of the true witness is filled by two realities— Jesus Christ, the ultimate and final reality, the goal of all things, and the persons who he desires should recognize that reality; he himself is no more than the one who calls attention to the link between them, brings into sight, so to say, the hidden bond which already exists, because Jesus Christ is He in whom and for whom and to whom all things have been created and the one through whose life and death and resurrection a new humanity has been inaugurated.[2] Moreover, the witness stands in essentially the same relationship to this Event as the persons to whom he bears witness. He has the same need of it; it does the same things for him. He does not stand in some superior position, reaching down to the person to whom he bears witness. He stands alongside him, pointing him to an Event which is equally decisive for both of them and in which both equally need to share.[3]

This kind of relationship, of witness in subordination to the other man, is possible only through the crucifixion. On the horizontal plane of human relationships there are impassable barriers to communication at this depth. On the one side, there is the natural human resistance to anything which appears to be an invasion of one's own selfhood, and on the other side, the natural human desire to put the other man under an obligation to oneself by giving him something valuable which he lacks and I possess. Neither party to the transaction can escape from these imprisonments of human pride by his own effort or determination. Only if there comes into that situation a vertical dimension to which both are alike related and to which both are alike subordinated does communication at the needed depth and with the needed openness become possible. The communication which is involvement with one another, with the defences going down, is only possible because between me and my neighbour there is always a Cross—a cross which crucifies and buries our isolation and self-sufficiency and is the door to a risen life in a new humanity. We come to know ourselves to be involved together in that new humanity, with openness to and responsibility for one another in a life which we partake of together or not at all.

This is why the real witness and the only true evangelist is the Holy Spirit. It is God the Holy Spirit who plants that Cross between me and my neighbour. It is He who can thereby take my efforts to reach across the gulf of selfhood to the other person, and by taking them up into Jesus Christ crucified and risen, use them to speak to the man on the other side of the gulf. Every "telling of the name" which is more than mere sounds is a miracle of the Holy Spirit.

All this, it may be noted, is nothing more than a comment on Paul's account of his relations in the Gospel with the Corinthians:[4] "It is not ourselves that we proclaim: we proclaim Christ Jesus as Lord, and ourselves as your servants, for Jesus' sake." Your servants—your bondservants, slaves, *douloi*. . . . Not, be it noted, "for your sake" but "for Jesus' sake": the bond is not simply one of human solidarity, it is the bond of the new humanity in Jesus Christ. The emphasis of the whole passage is on dying to ourselves that the life that is in Jesus Christ may reveal itself. "Wherever we go we carry death with us in our body, the death that Jesus died, that in this body also life may reveal itself, the life that Jesus lives. For continually, while still alive, we are being surrendered into the hands of death, for Jesus' sake, so that the life of Jesus also may be revealed in this mortal body of ours. Thus death is at work in us, and life in you"[5]—the death, we may say, of our own selfhood that the life of Jesus may be at work in you.

Some consequences follow regarding the form of mission. Before there can be witness in any explicit fashion, a human relationship must be established, a relationship which recognizes and expresses our common humanity and so provides the setting in which communication at the deeper level, within the "vertical" dimension, so to speak, becomes possible. It is necessary to recognize fully and genuinely the selfhood of the other person, his essential humanity, before we have the right to testify to him of the Gospel. This is so because of the nature of the Gospel which affirms that selfhood and at the same time makes possible its liberation into its true fulfilment in the new

83

humanity in Christ. Or to put it from the other side, we must recognize the reality of our common creation in Christ before we are in a position to speak to others about our re-creation in Him.[6]

The necessity for the establishment of this relationship within a common humanity, as a necessary precondition of witness to the Event which inaugurates a new humanity, may be thought so obvious as scarcely to merit mention. And yet there have been those engaged in missions (in their own countries as well as abroad) who have been so seized of the urgency of proclaiming Christ that they have not taken time to establish such a human relationship before embarking on the attempt to testify to the Event. This would seem to ignore the necessity for the "*doulos*-relationship" of which Paul speaks, and so to make any effective communication of the Gospel impossible.

The point, however, cuts deeper than this superficial misunderstanding of the nature of mission as witness. It implies that witness in this sense is witness to men as persons, to men in their basic humanity, and not to systems of thought or to social structures as such. Mission as witness is mission primarily to men as men, and not primarily as Hindus, Muslims, Marxists, scientific humanists or whatever the religious framework of their living may be, nor primarily to them as farmers, factory workers, or members of the managerial or professional groups or whatever the occupational framework of their living may be. This is not to say that mission must not find its expression—even in organizational forms—within the different religious and occupational frameworks within which men live. On the contrary, it is one of the convictions of this essay, that such frameworks, which are the milieux within which men realize and express their humanity, need to be taken more seriously by Christian missions than they have often been in the past. Nor is it to say that missions do not need to learn the "language" of such religious and occupational frameworks—the thought-forms which are appropriate to them, the traditions they embody, the psychological attitudes which they engender, the sociological trends to which they are subject and which they express and to which they give direction. On the contrary, the understanding of the "language" of these frameworks is essential equipment for establishing that relationship within a common humanity which we hold to be an essential precondition of witness. A vast amount of thought and experiment by Christians is needed in this sphere.

But it is contended that the purpose of such planting of missions within the varied frameworks of human living and the learning of their "languages" is to enable Christian witness to be made to men as persons, to penetrate through the layers of relationships within which men live their lives, to the living centre into which those relationships are gathered, to what makes a man a man. For it is at this living centre, whether a man recognizes it or not, that God addresses him directly, and it is in that address that he is given the possibility of being a real person. This is again to say that the final witness is the Holy Spirit, for only He can penetrate into the living centre of a human person.

The point is of importance also as a means of purifying the motives which lead us to engage in mission. If the purpose of mission as witness is to testify of the Event of Jesus Christ to men as men, then it is with men *because they are men* that missions are concerned. It is not with men for some other reason: for example, as objects of our pity. The fact that missions have in the last century commonly been from higher income groups to lower income groups has led to great confusion at this point. (It should be noted that this has been the case with missions in the home countries as well as missions abroad.) It has presented a picture of mission as a concern on the part of the privileged for the underprivileged. But the material status of men has nothing whatever to do with mission as witness. Whether a man or a community is rich or poor in this world's goods has nothing to do with their need to know the name of their Redeemer (save in so far as it may be harder for the rich man or community to hear that name).[7] Whether a Christian or a church is rich or poor has nothing to do with their responsibility to witness to that name. Whether the person who tells me that name is rich or poor makes no difference to the value or reality of his testimony. To present mission as a form of Christian compassion felt by the privileged for the underprivileged is to distort disastrously the meaning of mission *and* the meaning of Christian compassion.

This is not to suggest that Christian commitment does not involve the expression of that commitment in compassion for those in need. On the contrary, as has already been noted (p. 43 f.), it is to assert that that compassion stands in its own right as one inevitable expression of the Christian life, irrespective of what may flow from it in terms of the ultimate convictions of those on whom the compassion is bestowed. Nor is it to suggest a final cleavage between the work of mission and the work of compassion. Christian commitment is one, and the Christian life is one. It is never a case of choosing between mission or compassion: we are inevitably involved in both. But it is to say that to mistake the one for the other, or to substitute the one for the other, is to harm both. And it is to suggest that such confusion has been prevalent in the past, exists to-day, and needs to be eliminated from our thought and practice if mission and compassion are each to find their right expression in the condition of to-day's world.

Rightly to distinguish these two expressions of commitment to Christ will involve some radical reconstruction of our thought and practice. For example, do we not, at least in the West, tend to think of "home missions" as an activity which is primarily directed either to the dispossessed sections of the community or to those who for some reason are social misfits? At least when we speak of "home missions" the first picture that comes to mind is not usually either of comfortable suburbia or of the intellectual *élite* of a community. But such distinctions in terms of economic position or social conformity or intellectual status have nothing to do with men's need to hear the name of their Redeemer (though they may have much to do with the ways in which missions ought to be speaking that name). The confusion between mission and compassion has not a little to do with this false limitation of mission to the economically and socially dispossessed. It may also have a good deal to do with the social stratification of denominations in some Western societies. We may be thankful for the many signs that Christians in the West are beginning to free themselves from the consequences of this past confusion and to discover ways of participating in Christ's Mission to men as men in all sections of the community, whatever their economic or social status. But a great deal remains to be done before the members of churches as a whole come to understand mission within the communities in which they are set as mission to men as men.

The same confusion has been apparent in "foreign" missions, which have all too often been thought of and presented to their supporters as the transmission of the benefits of an "advanced" way of life to a less advanced. The expression of this has taken different forms which have varied in their degree of sophistication, from the person who gave a subscription to foreign missions simply out of compassion for people who had less food or less medical service than himself, to much more elaborate arguments about the responsibility of members of nations who enjoyed such privileges as scientific knowledge, parliamentary democracy, universal primary education and a knowledge of Christianity towards those who lacked these things. The confusion was made the easier by the fact that, apart from government and trade contacts, the missions were in most areas the only channel of relationships between people in the one area (in which Christianity was the dominant religion) and those in the other (in which some other religion was dominant). Missions were therefore the channel along which both Christian compassion and Christian mission flowed. It was therefore almost inevitable that the word "missions" should acquire a connotation which included both mission and compassion.

In the radically changed world of to-day, the resultant image of "missions" is attacked from all sides, from the unsophisticated wish "to go and do a job where there is need provided it isn't connected with missions" to the highly sophisticated arguments that missions have been consciously or unconsciously instruments of Western dominance. (It may be noted that similar reactions obtain with reference to home missions, from those who dismiss them as "buns and the Gospel for the poor" to those who see in them instruments for the preservation of the privilege of a ruling class.) Nothing would be easier at this point than to throw out the baby along with the bath water. The process of disentangling mission from compassion and both from the political and sociological conditioning of a bygone age involves wrestling with firmly rooted habits of thought, long established institutions and deeply treasured relationships, all of which involve strongly felt emotions. It will not be accomplished easily, by slogans, or changes in nomenclature, or alteration of the externals of organizations, for it goes deep enough to require a new apprehension (which is more than mental understanding) of the relationship of Christians to mankind and its human groupings, and new forms for the expression of that relationship in terms of both compassion and mission.

So far as missions are concerned, the starting point in that process may perhaps be a rigorous and honest attempt to disentangle in their thinking their own distinctive task as missions from the task required by Christian compassion, not primarily in organizational terms but primarily in terms of the motives and purposes underlying their task as mission, and then to be equally rigorous and honest in scrutinizing their activities to see how far they are in fact consonant with that purpose, and their presentation of themselves to their supporters and to those among whom they work to see how far the "image" of themselves which they present to the general public is consonant with that purpose. The question of whether any of their present activities can or should be transferred to other organizations is, at least logically, a subsequent and secondary process, though it may well be that events will not wait on logic.

If one may judge from the way foreign missions have spoken about themselves and from some acquaintance with the reasons given for either accepting or rejecting service with them, it seems fairly clear that the motives appealed to in seeking recruits for the service of missions, and evident in the response to that appeal, have included many others besides those springing from an understanding of mission as proclamation and witness. (This may well be true also of home missions, but the writer does not know enough about their situation to judge.) One motive has undoubtedly been the sense of possessing more of this world's goods or of living in a privileged form of society, leading to a belief that this imposes an obligation to serve those who have less or are less privileged. This is undoubtedly a motive which springs from commitment to Christ and a sound reason for being led to some form of Christian action. But it is not *in itself* a motive for engagement in mission (though it may well lead on to such a motive).

Again, there have been times when those who have felt called to go deeper in their Christian commitment and who have sought for a sphere of activity which would demand a more heroic and total religious commitment than their present way of life have turned almost inevitably to missions. In more settled and stable days in the past, in the West, the only form of Christian activity which appeared to meet this need was foreign missions (at least in Protestantism: it has been pointed out that foreign missions provided an activity within Protestantism which served many of the same functions as monasticism in Roman Catholicism, in providing an outlet for a desire to be totally committed to the "religious" life). Again, the desire for such total commitment, if it springs from love of Jesus Christ and not primarily from a desire for one's own moral perfection, is certainly a Christian motive, though one may wish to ask questions about whether such total commitment necessarily means engagement in full-time "religious" activity: but it is not in itself a motive for engagement in mission.

In the process of disentanglement which is required, it may help to hold steadily in view the fact that the purpose of mission is to proclaim and bear witness to the Christ-event in such a way that men may come to know the name of their Redeemer. Mission is concerned, as we have already said, with two realities, the reality of Jesus Christ and the reality of the other man as a fellow human being. Its basis therefore does not lie in the motives of the persons engaged in it. It does not happen just because some Christians have a bad conscience about their economically favoured position, or about the needs of the hungry or the suffering, or about their failure hitherto to find ways of total religious commitment, and look around for ways of discharging their conscience. Much activity may result from the discharge of bad consciences, but it is not mission. Mission happens when men respond to God's call to be witnesses to Jesus Christ. It is something God causes to happen. Men's motives are significant only in so far as they may be some indication, along with others, to the candidates' committees and church authorities as to whether a man is in fact responding to a call of God to engage in Christ's Mission or whether he is (consciously or not) seeking involvement in missions for some other reason.

Similar considerations apply with regard to the second reality, the other man, as a fellow human being. Mission happens in the encounter between God and the other man

—an encounter which mission makes explicit and articulate. Missions must therefore hold steadily before themselves and before those from whom they seek support the fundamental importance of this encounter and a concern with men simply as human beings. The need to which they appeal is the need of all men to know the name of their Redeemer. The justification of their activity is simply that they seek to be at God's disposal to meet *that* need. In the course of seeking to meet that need, other things may be involved, but if those other things are allowed to become primary, or are used as justification for missions' activities, then the essential purpose of mission will be lost, or at least submerged.

The realization that mission happens between the two realities of God and the other man will impose a self-limitation on the activities of missions. "Every decision in life," it has been said, "is an act of self limitation".[8] This is implicit in the very word "choice". If missions choose to be mission, then that choice is a self-limitation to those activities which serve the purpose of mission. That means, among other things, a limitation to those activities which point to Jesus Christ, and away from ourselves and "our" mission. There is surely a sense in which a mission must be essentially unobtrusive—not, indeed, secretive, but existing openly and quietly and without calling attention to itself, in the "dimension" between God and the other man. It may well be necessary for it to refuse offers to provide it with resources or spheres of work which are commended to it on the ground that they will "enable it to exercise a great influence", just because it is not its job to exercise an influence in that sense, and to be tempted to do so would be to point to itself instead of to Jesus Christ. It must certainly reject any temptation to use the "powers of the present age" as means of influencing men to a commitment to Jesus Christ or even for its own protection, for it then becomes not a witness in the dimension of God's encounter with the other man, but an instrument of a political or sociological or economic force in the "horizontal" dimension of human relationships.

It is foolish to be merely Utopian about this. Missions are, in one aspect, human organizations existing in time and space. If they were not, they could not testify to the Christ-event which happened *in* history, or be the human, historical link with that event. They can never escape from the fact that as such they exist as sociological entities and have political and social and economic consequences. It is one thing, however, to recognize the fact and to seek to be responsible in regard to it, so that the existence of a mission as a sociological entity may not contradict its witness as mission. It is quite another thing to use political or social or economic pressure as an instrument of mission. That is both to fail to respect the selfhood of the other man and to suppose that commitment to Jesus Christ takes place in the horizontal dimension as a result of human action, and not in the vertical dimension as a result of the action of God the Holy Spirit.

Certainly, the Utopianism which pretends that missions are not institutions in this historic aeon and therefore are not subject to the infections of human pride and rebelliousness and self-will is to be avoided; if it is not, those infections will be all the more dangerous because they will be unobserved by those engaged in the mission (though not by outside observers!). But it may preserve missions from falling into the opposite error of engaging in a kind of ecclesiastical power politics if they constantly remind themselves that the basic form of witness is "presence"—to exist in a situation with a sense of responsibility towards men in it, and with the constant intention of witness to the Christ-event within it. That is the essential form of mission.

Such "presence" is prior to any activity. The first result of commitment to Jesus Christ is to receive the new quality of life that is His gift, and to live it. In that sense, being is prior to doing in the Christian life. Mission is presence before it is action—the presence in any human situation of those who live by the new life in Christ and so are by their very presence witnesses to the new creation. In that sense also passivity comes before activity in the Christian life. Mission is the passivity of being at God's disposal before it is the activity of any deliberate act of witness. The "presence" of a Christian community with a quality of life within it that is unmistakably the "life of a new age" inevitably provokes cross-examination: and cross-examination provides the right occasion—perhaps the only fully right occasion—for witness.

PART II

CHAPTER 8

WHERE IS THE FRONTIER?

THE FIRST PART OF THIS ESSAY HAS OFFERED SOME comments on the meaning of mission from the ground of the testimony of Scripture. In this second part, we shall examine in the light of those comments some of the questions arising from the present situation of missions.

The basic image evoked by the word "missions" in the minds of many of those who are engaged in missions and of those who support missions is of groups of Christians being sent from one area of the world to another to proclaim the Christian Gospel. This image carries with it the implication that in the process the Christians so sent cross some kind of boundary between the group from which they are sent and the group to which they are sent. Many of the questions which are engaging the attention of those who think about missions to-day are, in one form or another, questions about this boundary. Is there such a boundary to be crossed? If so, what is its nature and where is it located?

Questions of this kind have arisen particularly in the sphere of foreign missions in the form they have taken in the last two centuries. The generally held, broad picture of their activity has been of Christians being sent from within an area designated "Christendom" to "the non-Christian world". These concepts (Christendom and the non-Christian world) had both a geographical and a cultural content. Christendom could, to some extent at least, be marked on the map. It had a geographical "frontier". If that frontier (like some political frontiers) could not be too precisely marked at some points, at least it was clear to most folk then concerned with missions that Asia, Africa and the Pacific were at that time in "the non-Christian world", and that missions were sent across the frontier of Christendom into that world. The sense in which the Western world could rightly be designated "Christendom" with the meaning that its current cultural standards and practices were controlled by the Christian Gospel was even more uncertain: but at least it seemed clear at that time that Christianity was the religion of Western culture in a way in which it was not the religion of the cultures of the peoples of Asia, Africa and the Pacific. To be sent from the West to Asia, Africa or the Pacific clearly involved crossing a religio-cultural boundary. The geographical boundary and the religio-cultural one were both symbolized in the fact that thus to be sent involved making a journey and in the process crossing physical and political and cultural frontiers.

The resultant picture, of a group of Christians making a physical journey across frontiers to lands where the cultural tradition is radically different and where the dominant religion is not Christianity in order to proclaim the Christian Gospel, has become the stereotype of "missions". It tends to be the frame into which our thoughts about the meaning of mission are fitted.

It is not our purpose at this point to raise the question whether this form of an understanding of mission was adequate for its own day. We are concerned with the question whether the stereotype of mission which has been bequeathed to us from that day provides an adequate framework for the understanding of mission in our own time. The uncritical retention of a form of understanding of mission from a past age in a new and radically different period may obscure, rather than illuminate, our understanding of the meaning of mission and may hamper rather than further the prosecution of its task. Its uncritical rejection may result in the loss of elements vital to the

98

understanding and practice of mission. It is therefore necessary to examine this stereotype of mission as the crossing of a geographical and cultural frontier, in the light both of the conclusions reached in the first part of this essay, and of the circumstances of our own time.

The adequacy of this understanding of mission for our day has been vigorously questioned on the ground that it is manifestly at variance with contemporary circumstances. The establishment and growth of Christian churches in the lands once regarded as "the non-Christian world", the implicit or explicit rejection of Christianity as the central core of cultural life in the area once regarded as "Christendom", the critical scrutiny of and resultant radical uncertainty about the relation between religion and culture, have all contributed to a situation in which yesterday's stereotype no longer provides an adequate understanding of to-day's scene.

Some implications of that changed scene are being drawn out and gaining wide acceptance. It would, for example, now be widely accepted that "the home base of mission is world wide" and that Christians in all parts of the world are "sent" in mission into all the world, which suggests a very different picture from that of Christians being sent from within "Christendom" into "the non-Christian world".[1] Strenuous efforts are being made to adapt forms of organization and existing relationships to express this changed concept. Again—and this is perhaps less often noticed in discussions of the meaning of mission —Christians in lands once regarded as "Christendom" are increasingly aware that they too live in a missionary situation and are "sent" to proclaim the Christian Gospel within their own cultural tradition. This awareness is increasingly expressed in action, and, it may be observed, in explaining the meaning of such action, terms such as "frontier", "boundary" are widely used.

But is this "frontier" concept valid? Mission can no longer be described as the crossing of a frontier between a

99

Christendom conceived in geographical terms and the rest of the world, because Christendom, in the sense of those groups of people who seek to live under the Lordship of Jesus Christ and to express their allegiance in their corporate relationships, is now geographically fragmented, and because there is no country where the proclamation of the Gospel to those who do not know it or who reject it is not needed.

It does not, however, follow that geography has no longer any significance for our understanding of mission. The call to cross a geographical frontier, and to go out to a land not one's own and into a cultural tradition different from that in which one has been nurtured, has been one way in which Christians have been called to recognize and accept the reality of their being a "sent" people.

An answer frequently given to the question "Where is the frontier?" is that the Christian mission consists in crossing the frontier between the Church and the world. This obviously raises the whole much-debated question about the definition of the Church. For the present purpose, one comment must suffice. If by the word "Church" is meant a company of people whose membership is known only to God, then it may be true to say that mission takes place in crossing the frontier between that company and the rest of humanity. This, however, is not very helpful in understanding the meaning of mission concretely, because the frontier here thought of is, by definition, invisible to human eyes. If, on the other hand, by the word "Church" is meant the various existing institutions, the churches, then to say that mission happens in crossing the frontier between the Church and the world is to suggest that the churches as they exist here and now belong wholly to the new age inaugurated in the Christ-event, and to obscure the fact that they also belong to this present era, and are involved in its rebelliousness. The churches are both societies committed and open to the Lordship of Christ and living by the gifts of the Holy Spirit, and also human institutions. They cannot in this historical era escape this ambivalent character. To seek to escape from it means either to try to anticipate the consummation of God's purpose at the end of the historical era or to reject that consummation by denying that they share here and now in the life of the age to come.

It does not, however, follow that the view that the Christian mission consists in crossing the frontier between the Church and the world must simply be thrown away. It reminds us that mission is not merely an affair of individual Christians proclaiming the Gospel to individuals: it is an activity of a corporate body of Christians and is directed to men in their corporate relationships. On both sides it is concerned with men in corporate, historical and continuing structures. Mission is concerned not only with the individual and his contemporary decision for or against Jesus Christ, but also with the historic dimension of the cultural framework of human living.

A different answer to the question "Where is the frontier?", and one which also concerns home as much as foreign missions, appears when it is said that the essential form of mission is from the "saved" to those who are "not saved". This is an assertion which would be made by many who would not use this particular language. It obviously brings us near to the heart of the whole matter. If there is no distinction between those who know and acknowledge that they have been drawn into a radically new kind of life in Jesus Christ and those who do not know or acknowledge it, then Christians have no mission in the world, and the question about crossing a frontier has no meaning. Mission rests inescapably on the conviction that the distinction between those committed to Christ and those not so committed is the most radical and crucial distinction in our whole human existence. The issue for the individual, whether he is willing to accept incorporation into the new humanity for himself by his personal commitment to Jesus Christ, remains a life-and-death issue, and no understanding of mission which omits or obscures this element of personal decision can be adequate.

But to express the total meaning of mission in terms of crossing the frontier between the "saved" and the "not-saved" is to ignore the witness of the Bible to the fact that in God's act in Jesus Christ humanity has already been saved, the salvation of our human race has been accomplished and the new humanity in Christ has been inaugurated. It is to fall into an individualism foreign to the Bible, to reduce the act of God in Christ from a cosmic event to a private transaction with individuals, and to confine the activity of the Holy Spirit to the initial act of commitment, taking no account of His work in bringing both the individual and the human race into increasing maturity in Jesus Christ.

If, then, any of these frontiers are taken as the ultimate meaning of mission, they obscure its fundamental character. The basic character of mission, as the first part of this essay has attempted to show, is the being sent from Jesus Christ as the King of the heavenly Kingdom, the inaugurator of the new humanity, the "first-born from the dead". Mission is essentially from "the life of the age to come" into "this present age". The essential "frontier" is that between "the new age" in Jesus Christ and this historical aeon. Any use of the "frontier" concept which obscures this basic character of mission or equates an empirical frontier with this essential frontier will fail to point to the true meaning of mission and will distort rather than advance its true practice.

It is tempting, therefore, to reject the whole concept of crossing a frontier as thoroughly unhelpful. Yet the fact that its use, as we have noted, has kept alive awareness of essential elements in mission may give us pause. Is it pointing us to something which is more than a mere relic of a stereotype no longer useful, something which is still essential to a full understanding of mission?

An answer may be found by reminding ourselves that

the Christ-event, in which we have seen the basis of mission, was a coming into *this* world. Participation in Christ's Mission is participation in it within this historical era. It is in the setting of time and space that we are called to share in His Mission, and our obedience to that call must take seriously the conditions of time and space. To attempt to ignore them would be to dissolve mission into a vague idealism, which takes seriously neither God's deed in Christ nor the actual circumstances of our human situation.

In that human situation, men live in particular places, here and not there, in this cultural tradition and not that. Because of their historical circumstances they have or have not the opportunity to know Jesus Christ. They are, or are not, members of a church. These distinctions must not be made ultimate: but within the perspective of our human existence they are not to be ignored.

From this point of view, we may recognize a secondary sense in which Christians are sent in mission, and it is one in which the frontier concept may be found helpful in expressing essential elements in the understanding of mission within this era of time and space.

The crossing of a geographical frontier points to the need in the understanding and practice of mission to take seriously the actual, physical place in which men live, to be physically alongside men wherever they are, to proclaim Jesus Christ to them within both the limits and the possibilities of their geographical and their cultural environment. It is therefore a response to the commitment to Jesus Christ the universal saviour, and a witness to the fact that He comes to us men where we are. When some Christians are called and commissioned to go from their own countries and cultures to other countries and cultures solely for the sake of proclaiming Jesus Christ, they are bearing witness to the fact that Jesus Christ must be proclaimed from within every culture and country, that He cannot be domesticated in any one country or culture, and that wherever men are found, they have the right to know the name of their Redeemer.

The crossing of the frontier between the Church and the world points to the need in the understanding and practice of mission to take seriously the real (though not final) distinction between the company of those committed to Christ and those not so committed. It is to point to the fact that the new manhood in Christ is a corporate humanity, that it must be expressed in a corporate body, and that the new life which we receive from Him, we receive in company with and not in isolation from our fellow men. When some Christians are called and commissioned to go out from within the company of the committed to proclaim Jesus Christ amongst the companies of those who do not know Him, or refuse to be committed to Him, or are hostile to Him, they are bearing witness to the fact that the new manhood in Jesus Christ is a corporate manhood and that the new life in Him is given to re-create the corporate relationships of our existence as persons.

The crossing of the frontier between the "saved" and the "not-saved" points to the need in our understanding and practice of mission to take seriously the distinction between those whose lives are committed to Jesus Christ and those whose lives are not, between those whose living is "by faith in the Son of God, who loved me and sacrificed himself for me"[2] and those whose living is by some other faith. When some Christians are called and commissioned to cross the frontier between faith and unbelief for the sake of proclaiming Jesus Christ amongst those who are not living by faith in Him, they are bearing witness to the life-and-death character of the decision with which He confronts men.

The three "frontier-crossings" we have considered are not to be sharply separated from each other, still less set over against each other. They are aspects of one whole. To regard one of them as the whole, as though the whole meaning of mission could be understood in terms of it, would be fatally to distort the meaning of mission. For these crossings of frontiers in our actual world are not the fundamental character of mission: they point to it, and are partial and ambiguous embodiments of it in the conditions of time and space. When they are undertaken by some Christians, they are undertaken as tokens of the fundamental mission in which all Christians are involved, and as reminders to the whole company of their involvement, not as substitutes for that involvement. To this point we must return in considering the organization required by mission and the function of those called and commissioned to be missionaries.

To make these frontiers absolute is to be disloyal to the Christ-event. The frontiers of His Kingdom cannot be drawn on a map. The churches cannot be equated with His Kingdom. The boundaries between faith and unbelief are not finally discernible by human eyes and the full consequences of our choices will not be apparent until the conclusion of this historical aeon. But to ignore these frontiers is to fail to accept the responsibility of sharing in the Mission of Christ in this present era, to contract out of being His witnesses in the empirical world, to look for the possibility of being obedient to His calling to share in His Mission in some easier sphere than that in which He requires it, in the actual created world and in the midst of the confusion and uncertainties, the dividedness and oppositions of our human life.

CHAPTER 9

MISSION TO MAN IN SOCIETY (1)

W E HAVE ALREADY NOTED (P.60) THAT MISSION IN THE
sphere of human creative activities and its expression
in the life of communities raises some of the most baffling
theological issues. It is not therefore surprising that mission
to man in society raises some of the most perplexing questions confronting missions in their day-by-day activity.

How much of a mission's resources, for instance, should
be devoted in any actual situation to medical missions?
Should a mission continue to maintain mission hospitals
when a medical service is developing under a government?
How far is it a mission's duty to provide educational service, or to participate, when that is possible, in a public
educational system? Are there particular forms of educational work which are distinctively its task? What are the
responsibilities of a mission in a new and rapidly growing
urban area? Do they include any concern for such matters
as housing provision, recreational facilities, training in
home-making in an urban environment, and so forth?
How far and in what ways should a mission struggle for
freedom to preach and to convert? Such questions are perplexing in themselves, and are not made easier of solution
by the international dimension which many of them have
acquired with the growth of international institutions and
the international repercussions which result.

The answers to such questions cannot be "read off"
from any theological slide-rule. They can only be found in
the actual situations in which the questions arise in concrete forms. For one thing, missions have inherited from
the past a whole range of responsibilities in the sphere of

society, which they undertook when they were the only or the principal agencies of Christian activity in a particular country, and its only or principal link with Christians in other parts of the world. These responsibilities cannot be merely repudiated, nor can they quickly be transferred to other agencies. A whole complex of relationships, traditions, organizational structures and emotions have gathered around them, and thereby the freedom of action of missions is very much restricted.

Moreover, answers to such questions must necessarily be determined in part by the possibilities existing in any actual situation. What is the size and the position of the Christian community within the particular society in question? What is the attitude to it of the general community and of the government? What other Christian agencies, besides the mission, are at work in the area? Such factors as these have an important bearing on a mission's duty in any given country and can be assessed only in actual, specific instances.

Are we then to say that the answers to questions about a mission's responsibility in the sphere of mission to men in society can be given only *ad hoc*, as the understanding of the distinctive task of mission is brought to bear on the actual possibilities in any given situation? Up to a point, this is true. No one other than those who carry the responsibility for making decisions can really know all the factors involved and experience their weight and influence, and so be in a position to make a decision in faith. In the end of the day, concrete decisions must be made by those who have the responsibility for carrying them out, and living with the consequences.

Yet in our attempt to understand the meaning of mission to-day, to leave this subject there would be an evasion, a sheltering behind others' responsibilities. For if our understanding of the meaning of mission has any validity, it should throw some light on such questions, even though it cannot answer them in specific terms.

Two preliminary considerations may be advanced from the course of the discussion so far. The first is that it leaves no doubt about the responsibility of mission to be mission to man in society. All that has been said in Chapter 5 makes this conclusion inescapable. Moreover, the discussion in that chapter provides an indication of the kind of relationship to the structures of human society which is required for the discharge of the task of mission, namely a relationship which we there described as "involved detachment".

But, secondly, the course of the argument makes it equally clear that while mission to men within the corporate structures of human society is an essential part of the articulation of the Christ-event, it is no substitute for the explicit and direct telling to men the name of their Redeemer (cp. Chapter 2). However unfashionable, unpopular, difficult or apparently unrewarding the task may appear, and however varied the circumstances within which and the methods by which it is done, the telling of the name of the Redeemer is at the living heart of mission.

Perhaps we can now go on from these two considerations to see that they are not antithetical but complementary.

At the heart of the Christian mission lies the act of pointing men to God's act in Jesus Christ. But what God has done in Christ is to address men as persons, to speak directly to the living centre of their beings. It is in their response to God's address in Jesus Christ that men grow into their full and mature manhood. It is therefore the task of mission to penetrate through the external layers to men as persons, persons addressed by God, and to tell them the name of Him who liberates them into the appropriation of their full manhood in the new humanity which is His gift. That is why the telling of the name to persons, in their own right as persons, is always at the heart of the Christian mission.

But in our existence as men in history, we are always found as persons in relationships, as father or son in a

family, as a worker or employer in economic rela[t]
as a voter or political leader in politics. If missio[n]
us the name of our Redeemer, it must find us w[.....]
through such relationships, not apart from th[em]
attempting to ignore them. Certainly it cannot [.....]
level of those relationships. It can never fully tell the name
simply to man-as-father, or man-as-employer, or man-as-
voter. It must go on to penetrate these "layers" until the
name is heard by the essential man-as-person in the living
centre of his being, in that which constitutes the essential
"I" who am father, employer, voter. But neither can mission reach that "I" by ignoring these relationships; on the
contrary, it must be inside those relationships in such a
way as to point from within them to their essential meaning for the existence of persons. Nor can it fully articulate
the Christ-event unless it is doing so in terms of its meaning
for the father, the employer, the voter, so that when he
discovers his essential manhood by response to God's word
addressed to him, he finds the significance of that manhood in terms of those relationships in community in which
his life as a person is expressed. Acceptance of the name of
his Redeemer ought to make a man creatively critical of
the structures and habits and standards of the society in
which he lives: if it makes him irresponsible towards that
society, then he has not yet come to know who his Redeemer is, or the height and depth of the redemption He
has wrought.

To hold steadily in view that at the heart of mission to
men in society is the telling of the name of the Redeemer is
to keep that mission in society in its right context. It is to
keep it in the context of God's act in Christ and of His
purpose to sum up all things in Christ. It is to bear witness
to the fact that "the government is upon his shoulder", not
on ours: that the ultimate control of events and of human
societies is in the hands of the God and Father of our Lord
Jesus Christ.

It is all too easy for missions, when they see very clearly

(and rightly so) that they have a responsibility towards man in society, to forget this. The temptation then is two-fold. On the one hand, it becomes easy to speak about their task as though the future of human societies depended solely on their activities—which, dispassionately considered, sounds as though they wanted to relieve God of His job! On the other hand, it becomes easy to address those who carry responsibility in human societies—the politicians and public servants, the scientists and technologists, the educationists and artists, and so on—as though "we Christians" knew all the answers to the immediate practical problems which confront them in their work—which, dispassionately considered, looks as though we wanted to relieve the politicians and the scientists and the rest of *their* jobs. To succumb to these temptations is to turn missions into propagators of an ideology. The defence against them is to keep constantly in view the realization that at the heart of the mission to man in society is the telling of the name. To point men in society to the name of their Redeemer is to tell them who is in final control: it is not to suggest that we are.

For to point men to the Christ-event is to point them not only to the act of God in Jesus Christ in history: it is to point them also to the fulfilment of that act at the end of history. It is to declare a kingdom which is not only hidden in this historical era, but which will also be manifest at the end of this era.

It seems to follow that a second element in mission to man in society, besides that of penetrating to the essential person within his relationships, is to strive to keep all human societies and their institutions "open", capable of response to the "end", to the goal of all things in Jesus Christ, to be a witness *within* them and not merely *to* them that their end, their purpose and completion, lies outside themselves. Again, these two elements are complementary, not antithetical, for the more open a society and its institutions are, the greater the possibility of that personal existence which arises from man's response to God's word addressed to him as person.

It may help us to move a step beyond these general considerations if at this point we pause to take a brief glance backwards over Christian history. In the light of what we have seen of the meaning of mission, we may be able to learn something from the past which will help us to understand the present situation of the Christian mission and so have a better possibility of seeing the way forward.

In the period of Christian history before Constantine, there were considerable differences of emphasis in the thought of Christians about their relationship to the community. It would, however, perhaps not be too wide of the mark to suggest that they conceived themselves to be a new "race" or "nation" dispersed throughout the Graeco-Roman world—a kind of invisible empire. Acceptance of the Christian faith brought with it a sense of emancipation, both moral and intellectual, which resulted in a new sense of community amongst Christians.[1] This was reflected in a detachment from human society which yet involved a sense of responsibility towards it. Christians began to think afresh, on the new basis of the Christ-event, about the meaning of human society. They began to serve society in fresh ways, both by communicating the Gospel and by serving men in society. The balance between detachment from and responsibility towards the community was tipped on one side or the other by different Christians (e.g. by Tertullian and Justin) and at different times in the struggle of Christians for, at worst, survival and, at best, recognition under an empire whose principle of integration was an emperor held to be divine. But it may perhaps be not too excessive a simplification to regard as typical of the central attitude of Christians to the community the oft-quoted passage from the *Epistle to Diognetus*:

For Christians are not distinguished from the rest of mankind in country or speech or customs. For they do not live somewhere in cities of their own or use some distinctive language or practice a peculiar manner of life. They have no learning discovered by the thought and reflection of inquisitive men, nor are they the authors of any human doctrine, like some men. Though they live in Greek and barbarian cities, as each man's lot is cast, and follow the local customs in dress and food and the rest of their living, their own way of life which they display is wonderful and admittedly strange. They live in their native lands, but like foreigners; they take part in everything like citizens and endure everything like aliens. Every foreign country is their native land and every native land a foreign country.[2]

We must recognize that alongside this attitude there was also a stream of fierce opposition to the Empire, regarded as a hostile power governed by demonic forces. Yet even that hostility is expressed with the idea of obedience to the state for conscience's sake, on the ground that the state is in some sense or other within the divine purpose.[3]

It may be noted in passing that Christians in this period were facing the question of their relation to one culture— that of the Graeco-Roman world. Despite the diversities held within that culture, it had a considerable degree of cohesion and coherence, with one legal system operative throughout it, one source of governmental power in Rome, and one dominant cultural tradition, the "classical" tradition stemming from Greek philosophy and literature. This culture was given a new vehicle for its transmission in the concept of *Romanitas*, and a religious expression in the cult of the Emperor. The problem of relating themselves to a diversity of cultural traditions with different centres of political power and different religious expressions, each claiming and successfully maintaining its cultural and political autonomy, had not yet confronted Christians—a fact which should be kept in mind if we are tempted to make too direct deductions from the thought and practice of Christians in the first three centuries to our own situation to-day.

The so-called Edict of Milan (313) altered the whole perspective of the relationship of Christians to the community.[4] Its objective was to secure to Christians the status of a "licensed cult" (*religio licita*). But its effect was much more far-reaching than merely to give Christians freedom to practice their religion without persecution or interference. In giving that freedom to Christians, it accorded it also to the adherents of all religions. Thereby it enunciated for the first time the principle of freedom of religious belief and practice. Even more far-reaching, however, was its recognition, from the side of the state, of the autonomy of a man's mental activities, personal beliefs, and religious practices. This is in principle more than the recognition of the separate functions of a "church" (in the sense of a public body organized for religious purposes, whatever the religion) and a state—the terms in which it is often presented. It introduces in principle the concept of a society which is not integrated round a single centre—a concept as strange to classical antiquity as to the societies of Asia and Africa which it reached through their contact with the Western world in the seventeenth and subsequent centuries, and one whose full meaning we are still seeking to apprehend. It is not surprising that the Edict of Milan has been described from this point of view as "a milestone in the history of human relationships".[5]

This separation of a whole area of human thought and activity from the context of political institutions challenged the Christian community to evolve and express in practice a social philosophy based on Christian belief. The answer of Christians to this challenge became the medieval system of the two spheres of Church and State, each with its own form of responsibility and its own method, but each recognizing its duty to the other and both operating within the one human society—what we might call, in the phrase of a later age, the relationship of the "dual mandate".

Certain features of this settlement call for notice. It was

113

a settlement worked out in a setting in which Christianity had become the predominant religion, not in a setting in which Christianity was encountering other religions. A fundamental feature of it, from the point of view of our subject, is that it is predicated on the assumption that the members of the human community concerned are at least acquiescent in accepting a political and social system based on an acceptance of the Christian religion. It is therefore able to assume the concept of a Christian emperor, who will both use his political powers in accordance with his understanding of the Christian faith and recognize the authority of the Christian Church within the community. The state thus becomes not the hidden or even rebellious instrument of the divine will, but its overt and explicit servant.

One result was the virtual submergence of the concept of religious freedom implicit in the Edict of Milan, until its reassertion at the time of the Reformation. But its reassertion then was not in terms of freedom of religion for adherents of other religions, but in terms of freedom to express different understandings of Christianity. Not until our modern era has the problem of religious pluralism within one human community been faced in any radical fashion. Christians have accepted the "we give to Christians" (*daremus Christianis*) in the Edict of Milan and have been all too prone to forget the "and to all" (*et omnibus*).

A second result has been that Christian thought about society, its basis and operations, and about the responsibility of Christians towards it has, until recently, moved within the framework of a concept of a society whose political and social institutions may be expected to express some definable relationship to the Christian faith and to be conducted by men who own at least a nominal allegiance to Christianity. When the question is raised—as it is now raised by practical issues confronting Christians in all parts of the world—"What is the duty of Christians in the corporate structures of human societies which are either neutral towards all religions, or integrated around a non-Christian religion?", comparatively little guidance is forthcoming from the tradition of Christian thinking since the third century.

A third result has been that acceptance of the Christian faith and assimilation to the cultural system of the "dual mandate" have, until recently, gone hand in hand. It is true that the cultural assimilation is on a different basis from that which had previously taken place in the Roman Empire or in the empires of Asia to other religions. The culture of the "dual mandate" type to which the assimilation took place recognized a focus of final authority outside itself, in the Christ-event, to which appeal could be made over against the cultural system.[6] Nevertheless, it is not easy to think of an instance, in this period, of Christianity planted in a non-Christian culture and evolving a responsible and creative relationship with it. The acceptance of the Christian faith and cultural assimilation went hand in hand.

It might seem that in this "dual mandate" settlement, the conception of the Christian community as the new "race" has become entirely lost—and with it, the awareness of the mission of Christians as Christians, as distinct from the mission of "Christendom" as such to the world outside it, of which the instrument could be the "Christian nation" as a political and cultural entity. Community "conversions" in Europe in the Middle Ages and the methods of Spanish and Portuguese missions outside Europe in the sixteenth and seventeenth centuries would lend support to this view. Yet that is never the whole picture. The conception of Christians as a community distinct from the human communities in which they are set, with a heavenly citizenship which implies a mission within humanity, was never wholly lost. The more radical element in the pre-Constantinian period, with its emphasis on detachment from human societies and its questioning of political and social institutions, continued both within the framework of the ecclesiastical structure and outside it, in the monastic movement, in the order of friars, and in the sects of the later Middle Ages. It was this strain in Christian thought and practice which made it impossible for Christians to be content for long with any settlement which wholly identified their heavenly citizenship with membership in the *corpus Christianum*. It may even be thought that the emergence of a double standard for clerics and laymen and for "religious" and "secular" clergy was a pointer to (though from our point of view also a distortion of) the double affirmation in the New Testament that the Kingdom has come but is yet also to come, and of the consequent attitude of detachment from, along with responsible involvement in, the life of human societies. That dialectical relationship was expressed not in the essential relationship of all Christians to human societies, but by having some Christians express the one side of it and the majority the other side—a kind of eschatological class distinction!

It is no denigration of the majestic sweep, the comprehensive conception and the rich devotion which went to make up the system of medieval Christendom to recognize (with the benefit of hindsight) that this reaction to the challenges of Constantinianism had within it inherent contradictions which were likely to lead to the breakdown of its "dual mandate". From one point of view that breakdown became manifest in the cultural revolution of the Renaissance and the Reformation, with its triple challenge to the medieval system in the interests of the rights of human creativity to freedom from ecclesiastical control, of new forms of political and economic groupings to freedom from political control, and of personal responsibility for religious convictions and commitment. Regarded from within the tradition of Western civilization, this cultural revolution was a decisive break with the past. Regarded in a wider perspective—and at a distance of four centuries— it may be seen rather as a re-arrangement of the elements in the pattern than as a wholly new attempt to think out afresh and from fundamentals the relation of Christians to human communities.

The less radical elements in the Reformation may be held to have transmuted the Constantinian settlement into terms of smaller social groupings than that of the Holy Roman Empire. Despite the new elements in it, Luther's doctrine of the Two Realms is basically the medieval "dual mandate" transposed into terms suitable to the emerging nation-states of modern Europe. Calvin's theocratic ideal is more radical, and yet it equally depends on the recognition both of the authority of the Church and the authority of Christian magistrates and is the "dual mandate" conception expressed in terms of societies in which the merchant classes were playing an increasingly decisive role. In England, the Elizabethan settlement is the "dual mandate" concept in English dress.

The more radical elements in the Reformation indeed challenged the "dual mandate" theory as such. They may be seen as the contemporary expression of the tradition we have noted in the earlier periods, of emphasis on the detachment of Christians from human societies and radical questioning of the institutions of society. Yet for the most part they still move within the concept of a *corpus Christianum*. Those who stressed the gathered church in the interests of having a church composed of believing Christians thereby pointed to the responsibility of Christians to be "colonists of heaven": but they still conceived of the community as in some sense owning a Christian allegiance, as their concern with "the duties of the Christian magistrate" shows. Even the most radical elements in the Reformation, the Anabaptists, the Fifth Monarchy Men, and the like, were still moving within the habits of thought created by the idea of Christendom. Their efforts to create a Christian theocracy, while on the one hand implying a repudiation of any responsibility towards human societies as such, on the other hand envisage a community in which the Christian population is co-terminous with the community: the difference from the medieval view lies in the view held of what constitutes a Christian, much more than in a basically fresh understanding of the relation of the Christian community to the total community. Such a fresh understanding could hardly be expected from a standpoint which was in effect an attempt to anticipate the end of the historical era! Reformation thought moves within the Christendom concept: the fundamental question of the relation of the Christian to a society which is neutral or non-Christian is not raised.

In the post-Reformation period, Christians found themselves increasingly involved with societies outside the Western cultural tradition.[7] They were ill equipped to formulate any guiding principles for the relation to them of Christian communities which resulted from the work of Christian missions. The natural result was to carry over into the entirely new setting the concepts inherited from the Christendom tradition—concepts which, however, were considerably modified in the process. There is need for a thorough study of the influence of inherited ideas about the responsibility of Christians towards the community on the work of missions of different ecclesiastical traditions in different parts of the world, and of the influence on those ideas of the human societies they encountered. Such a study could well provide most valuable materials for our understanding of the whole subject, and give our thought about it a wider perspective which it urgently needs. In the absence of knowledge of such material, generalizations are more than usually dangerous. We might, however, venture to hint by way of illustration that Anglican missions have tended to think in terms of a typically Elizabethan settlement in alliance with a Colonial power (e.g. Ceylon) or with the existing social system (e.g. Uganda) but have found themselves, in a non-Christian environment, driven in practice to the development of forms of church life which bear considerable resemblance to those in the tradition of the "gathered church". By contrast Congregationalists, for instance, working from within the concept of the gathered church, have found themselves in non-Christian environments compelled to accept responsibilities towards the total community (e.g. in Samoa and Bechuanaland) which made them in effect an "established" church and for the handling of which the concept of the gathered church gave them little direction or guidance.

Yet the questions which would thereby seem to have been put to missions received comparatively little attention amongst them. That they could be left so largely on one side was no doubt due to the impulse which played a leading role in the initiation of modern missions, that of Pietism in Continental Europe and of the Evangelical Revival in Britain. To a large extent, their attention was concentrated on the salvation of the individual and on acts of mercy and compassion to individuals, with attempts to remove some of the elements in the life of societies which offended their concept of "common humanity". In so far as they were concerned with the life of the human societies within which they worked, it was generally their hope that these societies would be transformed by the influence of transformed individuals, so that they would provide a milieu for Christian living in the way that Western societies were supposed to do. So far as they had a conscious objective for the societies in which they worked, it was, broadly speaking, that some day they should become "Christian" societies, i.e. it was the Christendom concept which governed their thought in this sphere.[8]

If this glimpse across history has any validity, one inference from it stands out. It is that the task of formulating an understanding of the responsibility of Christians towards the human societies in which they live is to-day laid upon us afresh and in an entirely new setting. For the first time in history, the Christian "race" is dispersed throughout the world and involved in a whole series of different human societies, which are informed by different cultural traditions as well as divided into different political entities. The formulations of the first three centuries cannot be directly applied to this new situation, for they were related to a single culture with a single political centre, though there is much to be learned from them about Christian responsibility towards non-Christian human societies. The formulation of the medieval "dual mandate" cannot be directly applied to this new situation, for it was related to a community which had officially "adopted" Christianity as its religious expression, though there is much to be learned from it about the responsibility of Christians towards the corporate structures of society. The Reformation formulations cannot be directly applied to it, for they too move within the context of Christendom, though there is much to be learned from them about the relation between personal and corporate responsibility. But essentially the elucidation of the relationship of the Christian minority to the human societies in which it is set, and its responsibility towards those societies, is a task still to be done, whose magnitude is only exceeded by its urgency.

CHAPTER 10

MISSION TO MAN IN SOCIETY (2)

HOWEVER FRAGMENTARY MAY BE OUR UNDERSTAND-ing of the total meaning of mission to man in society, the work of mission must go on: concrete decisions must be made, and cannot await the completion of our theoretical constructs. We may therefore ask ourselves whether the general considerations we have advanced, and the glimpse we have taken over past history, enable us to say anything at all about the issues under this heading which confront missions to-day. Without invading the sphere of concrete decision, where those who carry responsibility must make the judgments, is it possible to discover some indications which may assist the making of those judgments?

The attempt to explore this possibility is more likely to be fruitful if it is limited in its scope. Any signposts discovered in an examination of one area of human society may be relevant to others. We shall therefore attempt to examine, from the position we have now reached, the spheres of education and of the nation-state, to see whether we can discern any indications of the responsibility of the mission within them.

Education is something of a test case for the duty of Christian missions in the structures of human societies, for basically education is a community's way of transmitting its culture to future generations and at the same time one important way in which that culture can be modified as the result of changing conditions—economic, social, political and religious. It is therefore an instrument both of conservation and of change in a culture. Hence it is a particularly sensitive spot in any culture's make-up, and is likely to be a target for both those who are anxious to promote change and those who are anxious to preserve cultural traditions. The more self-conscious a culture is, the more sensitive it is likely to be about what happens in its educational processes. The most obvious of these processes is the formal education carried on in schools, and formal education is therefore likely to be the focus of these various influences.

When within this situation the Christ-event is made explicit by the Christian mission, the "horizontal" process of the transmission of the culture from one generation to another is, so to speak, interrupted. The Christ-event comes into any culture as a "vertical" dimension—a questioning it from outside itself. Because the Christ-event comes into history from beyond history, its articulation in any culture questions the self-sufficiency of that culture and compels it to face questions about its ultimate goals. It therefore checks the process of horizontal transmission of a culture through its educational process by introducing a point of reference from outside the culture. This naturally causes alarm amongst those who view the educational process as a means of conserving the culture. But it also puts questions to the direction of change. For education as an instrument of cultural change is still operating on the "horizontal" level—the change sought is a change towards new cultural goals within this historical era, and these in turn are questioned by the Christ-event. So again the articulation of the Christ-event in an educational milieu causes alarm amongst those who wish to use the educational process as a means of cultural change.

Let us try to make this line of discussion a little more concrete and look at it in the setting of, for example, a community in Africa. Prior to contact with the West, the community had its own methods of transmitting its culture, through the functions of the chief, through its religious practices, through its initiation schools, and so on. In the process there would be tension between the "conservationists" and the "modifiers", but the process would continue without radical questioning. Now comes the Christian mission. Some members of the community hear the name of their Redeemer, accept it, are drawn into the Christ-event. A Christian congregation results. A school is started. At once the horizontal process of cultural transmission is questioned. What is the relation of the culture which is being transmitted to the Christ-event articulated in its midst? At some point the "conservationists" will become active again and will want the school to be an instrument of conservation of the community's culture; the question then will be whether the conservation is to be secured by rejection of the Christ-event and reassertion of the culture so far as possible in its old form, or by a modification of that culture in the light of the Christ-event as understood. But at the same time the "modifiers" will be active. They may well want to reject the old culture entirely, to use education as an instrument of change, to alter the culture to a form of a Western, technologically-based cultural system. Again the question will be whether that change is to be secured by rejection of the Christ-event, and an uncritical acceptance of a technologically-based cultural system in the form familiar in the West, or by a modification of that system in the light of the Christ-event as understood.

This, we suggest, is in crude outline the kind of situation in which many communities in Asia and Africa and the Pacific are now placed. And the point to be noted in connection with our discussion is that the articulation of the Christ-event, when properly understood, questions both the process of conservation and the process of change. It does not allow either the culture known in yesterday, nor the culture hoped for in to-morrow, absolute and final validity, but brings both of them to a point of reference outside themselves.

This same situation in principle obtains in societies in

the West. The "conservationists" wish to see the educational process used to preserve the kind of culture which existed in the days before the advent of this technological era. The "modifiers" wish to see it used as an instrument to adapt the culture to the needs of the technological era. This is one of the crucial points in the current debate about the development of more scientific and technological education. In this situation also the Christ-event questions both the old and the new.

It is to be noted from these analyses that the Christ-event coming into every human culture from outside it, puts questions to any educational process, whether directed towards conservation or towards modification. It is not to be identified with any culture transmitted by any educational process. In actual situations, it is not easy to keep this steadily in view. In Asia and Africa (and especially perhaps in Africa) the articulation of the Christ-event in mission happened at the same time as the arrival of a Western technologically-based culture and to some extent (historically speaking) as part of the same process. Missions have had a very large share in the provision of schools through which that technologically-based culture has been introduced. There is in consequence a natural tendency to identify the Christ-event with the technological culture. There has sometimes been a tendency (amongst the "modifiers") to accept the religion arising from the former for the sake of getting the latter, and (amongst the "conservationists") to reject the former for the sake of resisting the latter. The realization that the Christ-event requires a *critique* of the technological culture, no less than of the earlier culture existing in Asia and Africa, has been slow to emerge, and its emergence has not always been encouraged by missions, which have not always been as clear as they might have been in distinguishing between the Christ-event and Western culture. Moreover, the distinction can never be so clear cut as it sounds in this crude analysis. The Christ-event has been one of the formative influences in Western culture over a long period, and in the complex actualities of any given situation of culture-contact it is not easy to distinguish the two concretely. There are, however, welcome indications that Christians in Asia and Africa are beginning to find in the Christ-event a standing ground for a constructive *critique* of both old and new cultures.

In Europe, the situation is almost the reverse. The tendency has been to identify the Christ-event with the older cultures—in some cases with the cultural pattern of the agricultural society of the Middle Ages, and in others with that of the merchant society which succeeded it. The emergence of the technological age has all too often been seen entirely in terms of a threat to a culture too easily called "Christian". There has in consequence been a tendency either to accept the religion arising from the Christ-event for the sake of preserving the older cultural tradition, or to reject it as an obstacle to the acceptance of a new culture based on a technical society.[1]

In facing the question of the responsibility of Christian missions in the educational sphere, it seems imperative to recognize unequivocally that no educational system can be termed without qualification "Christian", if by that is meant that it arises from and expresses the Christ-event. Every educational system is a community's transmission of its culture: it moves on the horizontal level. At any stage in the process it is subject to the "vertical" questioning of the Christ-event. What can be said of it is that it is more open and responsive to or more closed and resistant to the question addressed to it by the articulation of the Christ-event within the culture of which it is the instrument.[2]

It seems to follow that this situation is not fundamentally altered by the provision of schools under Christian auspices. Such schools will not provide an education which will arise from and express only the Christ-event. To do so, they would somehow have to escape from the historical order altogether. They will in fact provide an education

which is also part of the horizontal process of the transmission of a culture—some actual, existing culture. They
can do no other if they are to be part of a human society.
And that culture will be subject to the questioning of the
Christ-event.

This is not to say that the Christian community in certain situations will not find it both necessary and right to
provide schools for the education of its own children. The
educational system of the human society within which it is
set may be so closed and resistant to questioning from the
Christ-event that those who are drawn into that event may
find it impossible to allow their children to be educated in
its cultural system and may have to provide their own
methods of educating them by whatever means are open
to them. But it should be noted that such provision is not
for the sake of mission: it is for the sake of the existing
Christian community. It may indeed be an unavoidable
acknowledgment that the educational system in that particular society is, for the time, closed to mission. And if this
course has to be adopted, it is very important to recognize
that the education provided for the children of the Christian community is not immune to questioning from the
Christ-event just because it is provided under Christian
auspices. By that very fact it should be specially open and
responsive to such questioning.

A further consideration arises from the Christian's recognition of human creativity as a divine gift whose use in
freedom must be respected (see above, p. 51 f.). If this is
recognized, then the rightful, limited but genuine autonomy of academic disciplines must be respected. From the
standpoint of those who accept the Christ-event as ultimately decisive, this means that the responsible exercise of
that autonomy is one of the ways in which the various elements of a human culture are free to fulfil their true purpose. Thus for example, scientific inquiry responsibly pursued and with a responsible recognition that its sphere of
operations is a limited aspect of and not the whole of

126

reality, can yield a fuller understanding of the created world; since that world is, from the Christian point of view, God's world and since it is His purpose to sum up all things in Christ, such free and responsible inquiry is a service to God and not, in itself, in opposition to His purpose. What can make it an opposition to His purpose is where such inquiry is not free, but is made subject to ideological control either by a "religious" or a "secular" ideology, and becomes the instrument of the pretensions to absolutism and finality of any human cultural system. (And it must be frankly recognized that Christianity in any of its empirical expressions can become such an ideology.)

It seems to follow that an important part of the responsibility of Christians in the sphere of education is to struggle to keep educational systems open and free from ideological control, whether "religious" or "secular", so that, in the process of transmitting a culture, they are open to change, open to accept the results of free inquiry resulting from the work of academic disciplines whose rightful autonomy they recognize. This is not to say that educational systems are outside God's control, or are a matter of indifference in men's hearing of the name of their Redeemer. It is to recognize that God is in final control of the universe, and not man: that free and responsible inquiry is the use of creative gifts which He has given: that the control of the use of such gifts in the interests of an ideology is to try to put man and not God in final control: and that free inquiry, free from ideological control, provides the setting in which men have the possibility of responding to the Christ-event when that is articulated amongst them.

It is here that we may perhaps discern a pointer to the responsibility of missions in the educational sphere. May not their primary responsibility be to struggle to keep educational systems thus open, and to resist the imposition on them of ideological controls—religious or other? This is a service which will assist education to fulfil its true function in the life of human societies and so in the end prove itself a handmaid of God's purpose in creation. Such a service will help the educational sphere both to be truly serviceable to men as persons and to be a sphere in which men can hear and respond to the name of their Redeemer. In seeking thus to be serviceable to the community as a whole, and in so doing to seek to promote the conditions in which men can be more fully human, Christians may rightly expect the co-operation of non-Christians, who may also (albeit for different reasons) share the purpose of preserving educational freedom from ideological control for the sake of a more fully personal existence.

All this provides no direct answer to the questions which may be confronting a mission in any particular country. "Ought we to go on providing schools within the general educational system, or apart from it, or not at all? Ought we to be trying to put more resources or less into educational work?" For the reasons indicated above, answers to such questions can only be given in relation to specific situations by those who carry responsibility within them. But the foregoing discussion may indicate some points which might well be held in mind in making such decisions.

For instance, *so far as the purpose of mission is concerned* (and the limitation is important) it would seem to indicate that the most essential form of action is the sending into the general educational system of the country concerned committed Christians who are as well qualified professionally as possible and who go into educational service with a specifically missionary purpose. By that we do not mean with the primary purpose of using their place in the educational system as an opportunity for the conversion of as many individuals as possible to Christianity. We mean that their purpose is to teach whatever is their subject with a full respect for its integrity as an academic discipline (and if necessary to resist its subordination to ideological interest), to use whatever opportunities may arise in the consideration of the aims of the school or college or the educational system as a whole to express, in educational terms, judgments and insights derived from involvement in the Christ-event, and to be ready (and equipped) to answer the questions of "Why?" which will be provoked both by their class teaching and their participation in discussions in staff and other committees about the aims of the educational process. In other words, their missionary purpose will be primarily discharged in educational terms, within the educational sphere, and for the sake of education.

Their presence in the educational sphere may also provide opportunities for Christian witness as "by-products", so to speak, to be used in faith—and with tact! Their work will provide personal contacts which may be opportunities for "telling the name" in more personal ways. If there is a church at hand, that will give opportunities for service within it. Their presence on a school or college staff may give opportunity for Christian nurture of Christian members of the school or college. But, from the point of view of mission to men in society, in this case in the educational sphere, these things will not be the primary purpose of their being sent as missionaries into the educational sphere, nor does the need for their being so sent depend on the existence of such opportunities. (Note that "missionaries" here says nothing about their nationality; they may be citizens of the country concerned or of another country.)

It is recognized that this is a very different first priority from that which at present usually occurs to missions when considering their work in the sphere of education. Before it is dismissed as quite unrelated to present realities, let us be sure that some points are clearly understood. The question to which we are here addressing ourselves is that of *mission* in one aspect of human societies, the realm of education. We are not here asking about the provision of education for the children of a Christian community. In any given set of circumstances, as we have noted above, it may or may not be necessary and right for the Christian community to provide schools for the education of its own children. If it is, then let us not confuse the issue by imagining that such schools are provided for the sake of mission. They are not: they are provided for the nurture of the Christian community. It seems to us that the sooner we recognize that fact, the sooner we are likely to be able to see more clearly the responsibility of mission in the sphere of education. (The fact that schools provided by the Christian community for its own children may in some circumstances have to be supported with funds and staff from Christian communities in other countries does not alter this point. The fact that a school has foreign staff members and foreign funds does not of itself make it part of mission.)

Secondly, we are passing no judgments on the policies of missions in the past. What we are trying to do is to address ourselves to the question in the light of present circumstances and of what may be reasonably expected to be the circumstances prevailing to-morrow. It is increasingly clear that governments in all countries will provide more and more formal education at all levels. They may or may not welcome the participation of voluntary organizations in the provision of schools as part of the public education system: if they do, the conditions on which they will accept such participation may or may not be acceptable to Christians. But in any case the overwhelming majority of children will be educated in the public educational system. The choice before Christians therefore is either to regard the whole developing sphere of education as outside the work of mission (except for that fraction of the educational system which *may* remain under the direct control of Christian bodies) or to see the sphere of public education as a sphere into which the mission must go (in the sense which we have tried to outline above) and to utilize available resources to that end.

Thirdly, it is clear that to think in terms of sending missionaries into the public educational system does not in itself foreclose the question of the provision of educational institutions specifically for the purpose of mission. For one thing, such an approach presupposes a supply of committed Christians who are professionally well qualified and suitably equipped for the specifically missionary task outlined above. In some circumstances it is possible that the only way of securing such a supply may be the provision of a teacher training institution under Christian auspices (although even here the alternative of a Christian hostel associated with a public teacher training college, and perhaps providing a period of special training on completion of the professional course, would be well worth considering). Nor should this priority be regarded as necessarily exhausting the possibilities for the mission in this sphere. Circumstances may be such as to make it possible and desirable, for example, to maintain a limited number of schools under Christian auspices as places in which there is a special openness to the judgment of the Christ-event, or to provide a college under Christian auspices on a university campus. The point it is desired to emphasize, however, is that, so far as mission is concerned, it is penetration into the public education system and service within it that is of prime importance.

Fourthly, it must be repeated that what is here offered is *not* a policy for missions in education which, even if approved, could be automatically applied in all situations. There are countries where the educational system is such that it would be impossible for Christian teachers to enter it with a missionary purpose such as is described here. There may well be more in the future. What is here offered is the kind of indication of an objective to be pursued as circumstances permit, to which we are driven in the attempt to apply the logic of our argument in the sphere of education.

Finally, the reader who is inclined to dismiss this line of approach may not unfairly be asked to produce a better alternative. In the light of the preceding argument such an alternative would need to satisfy the following conditions.

It must not confuse the articulation of the Christ-event with the transmission of a particular culture. It must take seriously God's gift of creative powers to man and the rightful though limited autonomy of the spheres of human creativity. It must provide ways in which, within those spheres, a Christian witness can be borne to God's purpose to sum up all things in Christ. It must not claim for Christians any rights which it is not also prepared to claim for all men. And it must do these things in a way which will leave open the possibility for those engaged in the Christian mission in these spheres, as opportunity arises, to tell men the name of their Redeemer. Such seem to be the conditions which must be fulfilled by the Christian mission to men in society.

We may now turn to the examination of the responsibility of the Christian mission towards national states, to see whether this line of approach is confirmed or modified when a different sphere of the life of man in society is examined.

On this subject we need a special effort to move beyond the habits of thought engendered by the medieval "dual mandate" settlement (see above, p. 113). The Christian mission, as we noted in our glimpse across history, is now confronted by the necessity of discovering its proper relationship towards, and its creative role within, a whole range of nation-states. The majority of their inhabitants do not own allegiance to Jesus Christ. All of them at present claim complete political autonomy. Their cultural traditions are many and varied (despite a "top-dressing" of the technological culture of the twentieth century). In this situation, to look for a "dual mandate" of church (of some religion or other) and state on the basis of the integration of the community around a common religion is manifestly impracticable. It is also, if the argument of this essay is sound, from the Christian point of view theologically mistaken. It does not take seriously enough the fact that the Christ-event transcends the historical order, and therefore no churches in history and no states in history can fully embody or express it. Nor does it take sufficiently seriously the autonomy of spheres of human creativity, including the political sphere. It does not recognize the fact that the centre of the final loyalty of Christians is beyond the historical order, and that therefore the Christian community is always distinct from the community of any human society (however many professing Christians there may be in the latter). It is also dangerous, because it opens the way to a messianic totalitarianism, based on the alliance of a religion (as a cultural phenomenon) with a nation-state. The natural answer to any claim to be a "Christian state" is the claim to be an "Islamic state", a "Buddhist state", a "Hindu state" or an "atheist state"; and there are plenty of signs that that answer is being given.

It is naturally tempting in this situation for the Christian mission to seek to contract out; to affirm that it is concerned with "religion" and has nothing to do with politics (except perhaps when some issue which it chooses to label "moral" arises) and to hope that it may be allowed to get on with "preaching the Gospel" without interference. This is a temptation to which many missions, with the strongly pietistic tradition within which many of them have grown up, are particularly susceptible. It is in practice impossible. The consequences of preaching the Gospel impinge on society at numberless points which a modern state cannot ignore. To take the simplest possible instance, is a state which includes, say, both Christians and Muslims to make Friday or Sunday or both or neither a public holiday so that men may be free to worship? It is theologically mistaken, since its implication is that the political realm is outside the lordship of Jesus Christ. It is also dangerous, because it also opens the way to a totalitarianism by which the state controls all aspects of human society, and the "church" (Christian or other) is left to deal with the heavenly realm so long as it has no earthly relevance.

If, then, both a theocracy (whatever *theos* may be in question) or an "ecclesiocracy" and a retreat into simple otherworldliness are rejected, is there no way in which the Christian mission can be responsibly related to the political life of the nation-state, while at the same time maintaining its proper purpose and integrity? The attempt to face this issue has driven us to the conclusion (at first sight a highly paradoxical one) that it is part of the task of the Christian mission to strive for a "secular" state. We are here seeking to use the term "secular" in its original sense, "of or pertaining to the world" (Shorter Oxford English Dictionary). We are saying that the state belongs to this historical *saeculum* ("age"). We are not thereby saying either that God has nothing to do with it, or that the state itself should seek to advocate or impose any theory about the non-existence or irrelevance of God. We are saying on the one hand, that the state should be free from ecclesiastical control (whether the *ecclesia* is Christian or Islamic or atheistic or any other) and on the other hand, that it should recognize its limitation to this historical age; it is therefore relative and temporary and not absolute and final.

This, as far as we can see, is the position necessarily required by belief in the Christ-event as an event which comes into history from beyond history and by the belief that it is God's purpose to sum up all things in Christ. Taken together, these imply that, on the one hand, all institutions in the historical order are relative and temporary: and on the other hand, that in the fulfilment of their proper purpose within the historical order they serve God's purpose and are "in the end" taken up into the "summing up" in Christ. It is when they claim to be absolute and final that they resist His purpose and destroy themselves.

If this be so, then it is part of the task of the Christian mission, where this is possible, to send missionaries into the service of the state, in a similar fashion as into the service of education, in order to strive to help the state to fulfil its true function of providing the orderly framework within which the life of the community can be carried on, and to resist tendencies for the state to seek to become absolute and final.

It is important to note the motives which should move the Christian mission to strive for secular states. The prime motive must *not* be in order that the mission may have freedom to carry on its own work. The conditions under which the mission must work are a matter for God's dispensation, not its own striving. If we pay heed to the New Testament we may expect them usually to be conditions of opposition.[3] At least we ought not to regard the comparatively favourable political conditions of the nineteenth century as normal.[4] The motive for seeking secular states is for the sake of humanity and for the sake of the state. Its aim is that men may be free to be themselves and that the state may be free to serve its true purpose and function. In this quest for the secular state, as in the sphere of education, Christians may reasonably expect the co-operation of others who do not share their beliefs about the nature of ultimate reality, but who nevertheless share the objective of seeking a proper but limited autonomy for the state. Others, besides Christians, may see that the recognition of the state's proper, but limited, authority provides conditions within which men are able to be fully human, and reject "theocratic" states as tending towards civil strife or repression and even towards a modern version of wars of religion.

But, while Christians ought to strive for secular states for the sake of humanity and not for their own sakes, we should also recognize that this is in fact the form of state which provides the conditions within which men can respond to the proclamation of Jesus Christ. For it is in such an "open" state that there exists the maximum possibility to respond to the articulation of the Christ-event—whether that response is one of acceptance or of rejection.[5] And this, not simply because in an "open" state there is freedom of choice, but because in its recognition of the limits of its autonomy and in its rejection of an ideological foundation, the secular state gives maximum place to other activities in society to exercise their own autonomy and maximum openness to criticism of its own goals, and so gives maximum opportunity to those within it who seek to bring to bear upon it judgments derived from the Christ-event.

It may be suggested in passing that it is in this direction that we must look for the basis of claims for religious liberty and for religious toleration. Christians certainly have no business to claim for themselves what they are unwilling to accord to others, and if freedom to believe, practise and propagate Christianity is claimed, then that claim must be made for all religions. Such a claim does not seem to us to be well founded on the basis of a human right, though this may perhaps be the ground on which it has to be commended in the contemporary world. From the standpoint of Christian belief, however, it springs from the conviction that the only absolute claim upon men is that of Jesus Christ: all human responses to that claim, whether conscious or unconscious, whether Christian or other, and all institutional embodiments of those responses, whether "religious" or "secular", are relative, partial and temporary. Men must have freedom within those institutions to make their own response if they are to realize their essential selfhood, which lies in responding to God's word addressed to them. This indeed may be a "human right" in the sense of a man's right to be human: but it is grounded not in his existence over against the universe or his fellow men, but in God's act in the creation and redemption of mankind. The distinction may appear irrelevant to the politician drafting a constitution, but it is of great importance for the Christian's attitude to the state: and in the end, for the state itself.

If the arguments here adduced for the contention that the Christian mission should seek secular states (in the sense we have sought to indicate above) are sound, then they apply universally. What is sauce for the Asian or

African geese is sauce for the European gander. The revolution required, not only in institutional arrangements within society, but in the mental attitudes of Christians in the West, is, to say the least of it, considerable. Yet we may fairly ask whether such a revolution is not needed if the Christian mission in contemporary Europe is to be rightly understood and rightly discharged, and if those who have been drawn into the Christ-event are to know themselves to be, and to be seen to be, the "new race" within every human society.

The primary method by which Christians seek to keep the state "open" is clearly through their discharge of their responsibilities as citizens of the state concerned. But we may ask whether missions, in the sense of groups of Christians organized for the purpose of furthering the Christian mission, have any responsibility in this connection.

In the first place, they must take seriously the social and political consequences of their existence and activities. To pretend that they have none is a sure way of allowing them to become a prey to the dominant ideology of their environment. By lulling the mission into a false sense of being insulated from the pressures and trends of human society, it blinds it to the necessity for constant scrutiny of itself and its policies and practices in the light of the Christ-event, to check the growth within them of purely ideological tendencies. It has often been those missions which have most prided themselves on "not meddling in politics" or on "preaching the Gospel and not becoming involved in social welfare" who have unconsciously transmitted most of a dominant ideology; for example in the case of "home" missions, the social *mores* of a dominant class, or in the case of "foreign" missions, the social standards and habits of one culture into another culture.

This taking seriously the social and political consequences of their existence may mean, for instance, taking much more advice from Christians who are expert in these fields as to the likely consequences in those fields of the new activity or policy a mission may have in view, and seeking such expert aid in carrying it out. It may mean giving more attention in the training of missionaries to the spheres of political life and its institutions, not in order that missionaries themselves should necessarily be engaged in action in the sphere of politics, government, and the administration of the institutions of society (though these may be spheres in which some of them are called to serve), but so that, in whatever form of activity they may be engaged, they may be aware of and knowledgeable about its implications in those spheres, at least to the extent of knowing the points at which they should secure expert advice. (The advice of experts will not necessarily be decisive, but it ought to be weighed in considering any course of action.)

Secondly, a more important responsibility for missions is to recognize their duty to help any who are brought to acceptance of Jesus Christ as their Redeemer to understand the implications of that acceptance in the political and social aspects of their living. To ignore these implications, or to suggest by silence about them that they do not exist, is to truncate the Gospel and to treat the convert as less than a full person. It is just irresponsible to be the human agency whereby a man is brought to the radical "transference" of the whole centre of his living from "the dominion of darkness" "to the Kingdom of God's beloved Son",[6] from the realm of the old Adam to the realm of the new Man, Christ Jesus, and then to leave him with no guidance about the meaning of that transference in terms of his responsibility as a citizen, as a member of a local human community, as a member of a family, and so on. This, it may be noted, is equally true of, say, an African in a territory on the verge of or having newly gained political independence, much of whose attention, energy and emotion may be concentrated in the spheres of his people's political and economic future, and of the rootless youngster submerged in the (to him) impersonality and meaninglessness of life in a Western city. If the new manhood which has come upon him in Christ is to have full and continuing meaning for him, the first needs to know what deliverance in Christ from the dominion of darkness means in terms of the surging political and social aspirations of his people; and the second needs to know what sharing "in the inheritance of the saints in light"[7] means for his life and the life of his fellows in a human group which has repudiated its past cultural inheritance and has discovered no substitute for it in contemporary society.

The right course of action of a foreign mission in this sphere needs peculiar delicacy and sensitivity to discern. To say it has none because it is foreign is to deny the solidarity of humanity in Christ: and it is another form of pretending that missions have no sociological and political consequences. Yet inasmuch as the mission is, in human terms, a guest in a (humanly speaking) foreign country, it cannot have the same kind of responsibility or discharge it in the same way as those who are citizens of that country. There is no general solution to this dilemma: the right course of action must be sensitively discerned within any actual situation. But it may be suggested that where a church exists, the responsibility for decision and action in the political and social sphere will rest with it. This does not mean that the foreign mission is relieved of any responsibility. It means rather that its responsibility will be to make available to the church in the country experiences in these spheres gained by Christians from other parts of the world. For example, in countries where industrialism is developing in a hitherto agricultural society, the experience of Christians in older industrial societies may well help to indicate points of need for special witness, dangers to be aware of, and opportunities for the development of more fully personal existence, as well as changes needed within the life and organization of the church itself. Moreover, it will be part of the work of the mission to assist the church in the country to bring its policies and practices in these spheres to the corrective and broadening judgment of the churches in other situations—an important safeguard against any surrender to the prevailing ideology in its own country.

Where there is no "indigenous" church, then it may be thought that the foreign mission must act as the church as fully as it can within the limits of its foreignness. In so doing it must be conscious of its role as trustee for the church that is to come, and in its decisions which affect for example social institutions must seek to put itself imaginatively in the situation of the coming church, so that as the church emerges, it may grow into a social structure in which it can recognize the responsible expression of its own life and witness. The sensitive tact required by the operation will naturally be considerable and will only be granted to those who are open to the graciousness which is in Christ and who recognize that the redemption which is in Him is not their possession, but His gift to humanity.

It may be asked: "Is not this indication of the Christian mission in society an indication of the responsibilities of Christians as Christians in their place in human communities, rather than of missions whether home or foreign, as such?" The answer is, of course, "Yes." The Christian life is one and indivisible, and in the last analysis its duties and responsibilities and its privileges belong to all Christians as Christians. The fundamental Christian mission to man in society is the work and witness of Christians in the societies in which their lives are lived. At the same time, because we are creatures of time and space, we cannot all be involved in everything everywhere all the time. There is both room and need for particular callings to particular tasks in particular places. There is room and need for those whose particular calling is specifically to serve in mission in different geographical areas and in different areas of human living. In what follows we attempt to say something about such a calling and the organizational questions involved. In our present context we may note that the responsibility of all Christians towards the mission to man in society could be brought to a focus, sustained and given insight and direction by the service of those who accepted a special calling to serve the mission in this sphere, who sought to be specially qualified for that calling and who had a particular responsibility to gather together their fellow Christians engaged in a particular sphere of human living for that mutual help in understanding the meaning of Christian living and witness within that sphere which we saw to be necessary (see above, p. 65 f.). In this sense the mission to man in the various structures of human society is the forerunner, the focus and the servant of the whole body of Christians.

CHAPTER 11

ORGANIZATION: MASTER OR SERVANT?

AMIDST ALL THE FASHIONABLE DENIGRATION OF OR-
ganization, anyone who is a servant of any form of
corporate human activity which can be described as an
"organization" must often feel that his place at the dining-
table of humanity is definitely "below the salt". If he can
also be described as a "bureaucrat", he has little option
but to crawl under the table. And if he is also regarded as a
"bureaucrat" in part of that undefined but horrendous
monster curiously known in England as "The Establishment", he may expect at any moment to be banished to the
basement.

Anyone who has for some time been engaged in the administrative service of the Christian mission may be for-
given for sometimes venturing to doubt the wisdom of the
Almighty in creating us as embodied spirits rather than as
disembodied ghosts. To such a one it must often seem that
life would have been much simpler had we been able to
communicate by some form of extra-sensory perception
rather than by committees, could attain common policies
by some bodiless form of inter-penetration rather than by
conferences, and were "as free as air" from the tyranny of
clock and calendar.

Our world is not like that, and to pretend that it is is to
quarrel with the nature of God's creation and at bottom
to deny the reality of the Incarnation. In a world in which
time and space have to be reckoned with as given facts of
our human environment, and in which our personal existence is expressed through a physical body, organization

is a necessity. The right question is not, "How can we get rid of it?" but, "How can we keep it the servant and not allow it to become the master of our purposes?"

The Christian mission is not exempt from these necessities. It needs forms of organization if it is to be carried on in the actual world. The actual forms and habits of the organizations devoted to missions need constant scrutiny in the light of the essential purpose of mission lest, by that curious self-perpetuating habit of all human organizations, they become the master—or even the prison—rather than the servants of mission.

This issue is put sharply to missions to-day. To engage in mission. it is said, is a responsibility of all Christians. It is one essential expression of our being as Christians. To have special organizations for mission is to obscure or deny this truth. The inference appears to be that the sooner organizations for mission disappear, the better it will be for mission.

We may agree at once with the major premise of this argument: indeed we would strongly emphasize its importance. The growing realization of the fundamental character of the "apostolate of the laity" in so many diverse communions and in all parts of the world is one of the most significant and encouraging features of our time for the Christian world mission. In its emphasis on the responsibility of Christians to recognize the sphere of their daily work as the sphere of their calling as Christians, and on the need for the churches to recognize that they penetrate the life of human societies through the dispersal of their members within those societies, this whole trend of thought and activity is pointing to aspects of the Christian mission which we have seen to be vital, namely that the Christian mission is an inescapable part of the life of all Christians just because they are "sent into" the world (i.e. human society as it exists in this historical aeon) from beyond it, and are forerunners of the new humanity in Christ. Perhaps in some of its expressions this trend has

143

tended to under-emphasize the complementary aspect of being a "lay apostle", the responsibility for the telling of the name of the Redeemer. Nevertheless, the potentiality of this whole development for the Christian mission is very great.

But to draw from this development the conclusion that organizations for mission are no longer necessary and may indeed be an encumbrance is to do a disservice both to the "lay apostolate" and to the Christian mission. This step in the argument is based on what seems to be a twofold fallacy: the supposition that what is the responsibility of the whole company of Christians needs no organization to carry it out, and the supposition that the existence of an organization for a specific purpose relieves the members of the whole company of Christians of their own particular responsibility for or participation in that purpose. Whether these suppositions are true depends in part on the nature of the organization, on the way it regards itself and conducts its operations, and on the use made of it by the whole company of Christians.

If we understand the Biblical witness aright, it is constantly pointing us to a form of corporate activity by the people of God which might be described as "the part on behalf of the whole". This is the nature of the people of God itself. It is called into being through Abraham not for itself but that by him "all the families of the earth may bless themselves".[1] When it rebels against or denies its true calling, a nucleus within it, the seven thousand who did not bow the knee to Baal, the faithful remnant, the Suffering Servant is called to discharge its true purpose and call it back to its true existence. This concentration on the part for the whole comes to its critical focus in Jesus Christ, the embodiment of the true Israel and the representative Man, the part for the whole of humanity, whose obedience unto death is "not for the nation only but to gather into one the children of God who are scattered abroad."[2] Those whom He gathers in His risen life are gathered not for themselves, but as the first fruits of humanity.[3]

144

This pattern of the part for the whole is repeated in the corporate life of Christians. It is this pattern which underlies all Paul's teaching about the diversity of gifts brought by the members into the service of the one body. This diversity must not be pursued at the cost of failing to discern the reality of the one body, or regarded as relieving its members from their share in the duty of the whole. The diverse gifts are given on behalf of the whole, that the whole may be enabled to fulfil its true function. In the contemporary life of the churches the Lord's Day is set aside for worship, not instead of the other days but in order that they may also become days in which their activities are offered to God. Prayers are offered by Christians not just for themselves but on behalf of all men. The ministry is given to the Church not for its own sake, or to relieve the other members of their obligation to worship, to pray, to engage in Bible study, but precisely to help them in those activities. Churches have choirs not, presumably, to relieve the congregation from praising God (though it may sometimes seem that that is their purpose) but to help it to do so.

This pattern of the part on behalf of the whole is deeply interwoven into the very substance of the Christian life. We may indeed see it as the only pattern which is congruous with God's acts in creation and redemption. A redemptive act which is to redeem mankind in the setting of the created universe must be an act within the limitations of time and space, with the particularity and concreteness that implies: it must therefore be in terms of a part, a particular segment of time and space. But if it is to be redemptive, it cannot be subject to those limitations; it is an action in the part for the sake of the whole. It is, as we have noted, redemptive by penetration, not by abstraction. It thus takes the created world, extended in time and space, seriously, and is thereby marked off from all idealistic forms of redemption which offer redemption by abstraction from the concrete and particular. But it is also redemption by an act that comes into the created world from beyond it, and does not allow finality to time and space, and is thereby marked off from all forms of redemption from within the created order. It is the part within the created order for the whole—and the wholeness—of humanity which transcends it.

If this be a true understanding of the redemptive event and of the pattern of the part on behalf of the whole which arises from it, then we can recognize the mission of the people of God dispersed in the world as that of being the part for the whole of humanity, called to live from within the redemptive event, and so both to be the forerunner of the new humanity and the proclaimer of the name of humanity's Redeemer. But we can also recognize the need for that people to have a focus, a point of concentration for that mission, not to be a substitute for it, but to be the part on behalf of the whole whereby the whole is helped to fulfil its mission. This, we may suggest, is a proper and necessary role for an organization for mission—to be a point of concentration and commitment whereby the whole people of God is kept aware of itself as mission, and whereby that mission is given concreteness and particularity and is preserved from being dissolved in abstraction or imprisoned in local and temporary particularities.

In previous chapters we have seen reason to believe that the existing organizations for mission require modification if they are to serve the purpose of mission in the circumstances of to-day. The line of thought concerning the part for the whole may indicate the nature of some of these modifications, especially in the sphere of organization. We are not here attempting any kind of blue-print for the future, but only an indication of the direction of movement. In view of the great diversity of history, structure and ethos of those organizations commonly grouped under the designation "missions", any such indication must be in general terms; yet it may serve as some kind of bridge over the chasm that too often exists between discussions of the

Biblical and theological understanding of mission and the forms of organization of missions. In any case this is no time for detailed blue-prints. When the right forms are being sought to express mission in a radically new situation, full of exciting new possibilities for the advance of the Christian mission in the world, administratively tidy schemes are likely to be constricting rather than liberating.

Let us then try to draw out some of the implications of this conception of an organization for mission being the part on behalf of the whole. We must limit the range of our consideration if it is to have any concreteness, and we may consider the implications for organizations in the West for foreign missions.

The first implication we would suggest is the simple one that organizations for foreign mission should recognize that they are the *part* for the whole; they are not the total mission. They are servants of the mission, not its total expression. Mission is not to be equated with what they do: what they do is to be judged by mission. It is perhaps necessary to make this rather obvious remark, since organizations for mission are not immune from the tendency of all organizations to self-aggrandizement. It is too easy for the argument to appear, in one form or another, that since an organization is for mission, whatever it does is mission and whatever is done apart from it is somehow not genuinely mission. This not only insulates the organization from essential self-criticism, but it restricts the understanding and practice of mission to what can be fitted in to its organizational framework. This is not the part on behalf of the whole: it is the part pretending that it is the whole.

If an organization for mission is to be a point of concentration on commitment to mission, it is very important that the focus of its activities should be clear and central. This is particularly necessary for foreign missions from the West. Since, as we noted earlier, they were in the past the only or the main channels for Christian action in the countries in which they were at work, they acquired many responsibilities which are now by no means part of the central task of mission. For example if, as we suggested in discussing the concept of "crossing the frontier", at the heart of mission there lies the being sent from the new age to those who do not know of it, then an organization for mission may well ask itself how far its activities are providing a point of concentration on that focus. How far are its resources of persons and money, of time and energy, being devoted to the proclamation of the new age to those who do not know of its existence, and in areas of human living where its existence is unrecognized or ignored; and how far are they being devoted to the sustaining and edifying of those who already acknowledge the new age and are seeking to live within it? Is the organization concentrating on the proclamation of the divine Event in Jesus Christ which has happened and into which all things are to be gathered up, or is it in fact largely occupied with transferring resources—of experience, skills, persons and money—from those areas within the Christian community which have more of these things to those which have less?—an essential operation within the Christian community in the world, but not the focal point of mission.

If an organization for mission is justified in existing in order to be a point of concentration on mission, then it must constantly scrutinize its activities in the light of such questions as these, and be prepared to draw the consequences in action. But it clearly cannot usually take that action unilaterally: it has a whole nexus of responsibilities and relationships which have grown up over the years, which limit its freedom of action and which it cannot merely throw aside. This means that if an organization for mission is to fulfil its purpose on behalf of the whole, the whole must help it to do so, by enabling it to concentrate its energies on the focal point of mission. The whole, in practice in this connection, means the bodies of Christians to which it is related at both ends of its operations. The Christians in the country from which it goes may assist it to concentrate on the focal point of mission by trusting it when changes are necessary, or may hamper it by nostalgically wanting it to cling to some traditional piece of work or method of operation. The Christians in the country to which it has come may assist it by being ready for new experiments and by seeing its significance as a focal point for their participation in mission, or may hamper it by regarding it as a source of support for institutions or activities which it has traditionally supported. If the organization for mission is to fulfil its task, it must take the responsibility for keeping before both bodies of Christians its central purpose, and securing their support for its discharge. It cannot acquiesce in immobility without losing its justification for existing as an organization for mission. But neither can the bodies of Christians related to it, without losing a witness to the dimension of mission which is essential to their healthy life as Christians.

There are now developing other channels between Christians in different parts of the world along which resources of experience, persons and money can flow. This is a development which seems likely to increase. It is one which we believe organizations for missions should welcome. It offers the possibility of transferring to these other channels some of the relationships and responsibilities which have hitherto been carried by organizations for mission, but which are not directly related to the central task of mission, and so bringing that central task into sharper focus. To attempt to resist this development on the ground that, because an organization for mission has been the historic link between Christians in two different parts of the world, it must therefore continue to be the only link is surely to misunderstand the real function of an organization for mission. There is nothing in the nature of mission to justify the contention that an organization for mission is the only legitimate channel of communication between Christians in one area and those in another. At the same time, the bodies which are concerned in the development of other channels need to recognize that if they are to fulfil some of the responsibilities which have historically been carried by organizations for mission, they will need to accept some of the conditions which experience has shown to be inherent in those responsibilities, such as a continuing and not merely a short-term commitment, an unreserved involvement in local situations, requiring knowledge of language, cultural tradition and persons, and a genuine respect for the selfhood of the local Christian bodies.

This view of an organization for mission as a part on behalf of the whole implies, on the one hand, concentration on the central core of mission, and on the other a wide, varied and close relationship with other parts of the whole. It is difficult enough to hold those complementary aspects in proper balance even in thought; it is even more difficult to do so in practice. The tendency is to concentrate attention on one to the exclusion of the other; either to be so concerned that mission shall have a clear, vivid, vital focus that an organization for mission becomes introverted, exclusive, narrow in its outlook and concerns and unrelated to other proper and necessary responsibilities of Christians; or to be so concerned that mission shall be seen to be the responsibility of all Christians, and shall so permeate all their activities, organization and relationships that any sharp focus on its central core and any embodiment of it in an organization specifically concerned to keep its "cutting edge" sharp is lost, and mission becomes submerged in the total activities and the general organizations of Christians—for "where everything is mission, nothing is mission".

To translate the proper balance between focus and relationship into organizational forms is a difficult task. There cannot in fact be any one simple mode of translation. Any piece of organization, to be effective, must take account of the historical links of existing organizations and the present patterns of responsibility and relationships, and these vary in different actual situations. Organizational structures which will serve living movements cannot be "read off" from a theological yardstick or an efficiency slide-rule; they must serve, express and extend living processes, relationships and purposes, though to do so they must also pay proper attention to the critical comments of theology and administrative knowledge.

It would therefore be merely doctrinaire to imagine that the form of an organization for mission would be the same everywhere. The organizational shape it will take will necessarily vary with historical, ecclesiastical and other circumstances in different parts of the world. But at the present time it seems to us that there is need to emphasize the two elements of focus and relationship, while recognizing that their organizational expression will differ in different circumstances. If the core of mission has no embodiment in organizational form, it will be submerged in the general activities of Christians and will soon disappear from those activities. A board or committee concerned with all the activities and relationships of a church outside its own country does not in itself fulfil this requirement, for it does not give organizational embodiment to the core of mission. A church in some circumstances may very well need one body through which all its relationships outside its own country are conducted. This may be necessary for efficiency of administration and avoidance of duplication in its own organization and for helpful, well-informed and practicable relationships with churches and other bodies in other countries. But such a body for external relationships is not the same thing as, nor does it serve the same purpose as the "organization for mission" of which we have been speaking. It will provide some (but not all) of the relationships that organization for mission needs, but it will not fulfil its function of being a focus for mission. An organization for mission would naturally be closely related to it, using fully its channels of relationship, making available to it such special knowledge and experience as it possessed, and helping it to be constantly aware of the missionary dimension of its activity. But to regard such a body for external relationships as equivalent to an organization for mission would be to lose the focus of mission, to obscure the fact that mission is both to the ends of the earth and in one's own neighbourhood, and to suggest that the criterion of mission is that it is an activity which takes place only outside one's own country and, in some instances, is concerned only with intra-ecclesiastical affairs, and not with outreach into the life of the world.

In other circumstances a church may well have a diversity of bodies through which it carries on activities outside its own country. An organization for mission will equally be needed, to be the embodied focus for mission, to remind all such bodies of the missionary dimension of their work, and to provide them with the distinctive knowledge and experience which comes from concentration on mission.

It is important to lay equal stress on the need for an organization for mission to be effectively related to the other parts of the whole. If that organization becomes isolated and introverted, it cannot fulfil its function of keeping the whole aware of mission as an integral part of all its activities. Nor can it bring to other activities of the whole the distinctive understanding and insights that come from a specific engagement in mission. Since mission is an essential dimension of the life of churches, an organization for mission must be concerned with the whole of that life; it can only be so concerned without obscuring its function as a focus, if it has effective two-way relationships with the other bodies through which the organized life of a church is expressed both in its own country and abroad. The organizational forms of those relationships will vary according to circumstances. That they should be vital and effective is essential if an organization for mission is not to regard itself as an end in itself, or as the sole bearer of mission —if indeed it is to serve as the part on behalf of the whole.

The relationship between mission and churches has been

much discussed in recent decades. We do not wish here to traverse again ground which has been much trodden over in past discussions. Both the results of those discussions and the argument of this essay lead to the conclusion that the consequence of the Christ-event is both the gathering of Christ's people into some form of church order and their involvement in His Mission in the world, and that there can be no ultimate dichotomy between Church and Mission, so that there ought not to be any ultimate dichotomy between churches and missions. The problems arise, however, in the sphere represented by the last clause in that sentence. Churches have developed institutional forms in a "Christendom" situation in which they have not been aware of, or not fully aware of, the missionary situation which is the true setting of their existence in the world. Something is said in a later chapter about some of the consequences for the understanding of church structures of this missionary dimension of the churches' existence. Many missions have grown up as historically the only or the principal expression of mission, and have only recently begun to think of themselves not as the whole expression of mission, but as its focal point on behalf of the whole body of a church. In this situation, it may be worth while to offer a comment or two arising from this understanding of an organization for mission as a point of concentration on behalf of the whole.

In the West, one area of discussion has been on the relation of an organization for mission to the governing bodies of a church. This constitutional form of the matter is one point of entry, but it is important chiefly as a point of entry. The issue goes much deeper than constitutional arrangements. Neither a board or committee of a church responsible for mission, nor an independent missionary society is inherently immune from institutional self-perpetuation and self-sufficiency. Neither the ecclesiastical character of the one nor the independent character of the other as such protects it from becoming an organizational end in itself. Both of them need built-in instruments compelling self-criticism in the light of their essential purpose to be a point of concentration for mission.

Moreover, a constitutional position as a church court does not necessarily guarantee that the organization for mission will in fact be acting as a focus of mission for all members of the church, though it may well be a valuable reminder of the responsibility of all church members to participate in Christ's Mission. Nor does a constitutional position as an independent society necessarily mean that it is *not* such a point of concentration, though it may well impose obstacles to its so acting and to its being seen so to act, and to its fulfilling all its responsibilities as a focus of mission in other parts of the church's structure. But the substance of this relationship depends much more on less overt factors than a constitution. On the side of the mission organization, it depends on such matters as the mission's presentation of its work to its supporting constituency, on its policy in regard to recruitment, on its outlook and practice towards the church in its own country in its structure and congregational life and towards the churches to which it is related abroad, on its whole temper and ethos, whether it regards itself as a self-contained and self-sufficient entity, or as responsibly related to a body of Christians gathered in some form of church order. A constitutional relationship may express and to some degree extend such a relationship: it cannot in itself create it.

If an organization for mission is to be a point of concentration on behalf of a whole, then a constant critical self-scrutiny is required to ensure that it is fulfilling this purpose, and that organization remains servant and has not become master. For example, appeals for support are not infrequently based on an appeal to loyalty to "our society", with or without an evocative epithet—beloved, historic, newly-formed. Such an appeal may be justified if it is unmistakably an appeal to loyalty to the essential purpose for which the organization exists. The sense of corporate and continuing responsibility implied is indeed one way in which an organization for mission fulfils its duty to be a point of concentration. But if it means that the organization for mission is regarding itself as an end in itself, or as identical without qualification with mission *per se*, then such an appeal is fatal. It is then an insulation from the necessary critical self-scrutiny and a perpetuation of an organization for its own sake. "Organization's" take-over bid at that point becomes successful.

Again, an organization for mission may, almost without noticing it, have its policy determined to a greater or less extent by the necessity of securing financial support. In a choice between two possible pieces of work, one may be chosen, consciously or unconsciously, because it will have a strong appeal in raising funds; or an action may be avoided because "our supporters would never stand for it". It is too simple to condemn this out of hand. In part it may be one form of the rightful check by the judgment of a wide body of Christians on the way the organization is serving its essential purpose. The necessary reference to a body of Christian support may be a salutary check on the whims and possible fanaticism of a small group within the organization. An organization cannot fulfil its function of being a focus if it can live in complete detachment from a wide body of responsible support amongst Christians. But if the money-raising value of a policy or action becomes the dominant consideration, if an organization for mission does only what it can most easily secure funds for, then it has ceased to serve mission: it has become a servant of the spirit of the age. "Organization's" take-over bid has again been successful.

As a point of concentration on behalf of a church, it is part of the responsibility of an organization for mission to see that other parts of the church's life are kept aware of their missionary dimension. This means that it must be so related to them that both its witness to mission and its knowledge of mission are made available to them. How

155

this works out in practice clearly depends on individual circumstances—the way a church body is organized, for example. But it would seem important to recognize that any dichotomy between home and foreign missions runs counter to the understanding of mission to which we have been led in this study. There is a sense, as we have noted, in which foreign mission is the essential form of all mission, since mission is participation in Christ's Mission which comes into this age from beyond it. But this does not mean that foreign missions are the whole of mission, or a "higher" form of mission. Administrative effectiveness may require separate organizations within a church structure for home and foreign missions, but if so, it is very important that they should be seen as parts of one whole and that knowledge and experience gained by each should be made available to the other. It is even more important that local congregations should come to know themselves as involved in the total mission in the world; their local evangelism—house visitation, home Bible groups, the witness of their members in the structures of their own society, and so on—are not a different kind of activity from the share they take in mission around the other side of the world, but essentially part of the same activity.

It is also important that there should be a similar interchange of knowledge and experience between an organization for mission and any body in a church structure concerned with Christian responsibility in society. Enough has perhaps been said in earlier chapters to show the ground for the reciprocal relationship between these two points of concentration. Here, attention may be called to the special knowledge which an organization for mission acquires and which it holds in trust for the whole body. If an organization for mission has been really deeply engaged in the proclamation of the name of the Redeemer to the point where the proclamation speaks to men as persons, whether in a particular country or in a particular area of human living, it will acquire a peculiarly intimate understanding

156

of that country or area of life, of the kind that comes from continued personal involvement with people in the "inside" of their personal existence. Such knowledge should be regarded not as a kind of expertise for the exclusive use of the organization for mission, but as a trust for the whole body; and the other parts of the whole should be ready to make use of it and to take it seriously in their own particular activities. This of course happens increasingly in some spheres in regard to the knowledge accumulated by foreign missions, for instance in connection with the churches' action in international affairs. It happens less frequently perhaps in relation to the connection between mission to man in society and Christian responsibility for the ordering of human societies. Do we lack the distinctive knowledge of what it means to be man-as-scientist, or man-as-industrialist, or man-as-artist because we are only beginning to see such spheres of human activity as spheres of mission? Can we rightly discern Christian responsibility towards the structures of those spheres without that knowledge?

Thus far we have considered chiefly the relationships of an organization for mission in the country of its origin. But an organization for foreign mission must also consider its relationships in the countries abroad in which it is at work. We make only one comment on this complex question, and we make it because it seems to arise directly from the conception of an organization for mission as a point of concentration on mission on behalf of the whole. If that conception is a sound one, it must also determine the role of the organization for mission in the countries in which it is at work. We have already argued that it should not be the only channel for the transmission of resources, and we may envisage a multiplication of such channels which will relieve the organization for mission of some of its present responsibilities and set it free to concentrate on this special function. No more than in its home country should it be regarded as the sole instrument of mission: this, as we have seen, is the responsibility of all Christians. Similarly, it will be responsibly related to the church. But if it is to fulfil its task, that relationship must be with the point of concentration on mission within the church's own structure. The foreign mission exists not to relieve the members of the church in the country in which it is at work of their responsibility for mission, but to help them to discharge it.

Its relationship should neither be one of detachment from the church (in which case it cannot be a focus for mission on behalf of the church) nor simple integration in the total church structure (in which case it ceases to be a focus of anything). What is needed, it would seem, is an organization for mission in the church structure of which the foreign mission becomes part—but only part—and to which it contributes its experience, service and concern. Other contributions from abroad for other purposes would go by other channels to other parts of the church structure. The organization for mission would, of course, be related to other parts of the church structure in a similar way to that already described above. Only by some such arrangement, so far as we can see, can the church in the country concerned have the point of concentration on mission necessary for its full life and the foreign mission be able to devote itself to its distinctive task of being a focus for mission.

In discussing the relation of an organization for mission to a church structure, we have necessarily had to speak of its relationship to one particular church body. This, however, is misleading, indeed almost false to our understanding of mission. For the "whole" on behalf of which an organization for mission provides a point of concentration is not in principle one particular denomination among others: it is the people of God in the world. It cannot be otherwise if what the organization for mission seeks to express is the meaning of participation in Christ's Mission in the world, and if what it seeks to bring to a focus in a particular time and place is the witness to the Redeemer of

158

mankind of the whole "new race" in Christ. In the present divided state of the churches, an organization for mission which takes seriously its responsibility to live on behalf of the whole can be responsibly related only to a particular denomination: apart from such a relationship, it cannot but act as a self-sufficient entity and so deny the "on behalf of". But if its understanding of this "on behalf of" is limited to that denomination, if it fail to have constantly in mind the true "whole" on behalf of which it acts, if it fail to take account in its actions of its responsibility towards the whole body of Christians, then it is denying the ground for its existence. This ought to be (but is not always) a salutary check on any temptation to act as a fully autonomous, self-sufficient empire.

One other aspect of this matter of relationships between an organization for mission and a church seems in danger of being overlooked to-day. To be a focus of mission on behalf of the whole is not only to provide a point of concentration for a function which is one essential function of the whole. It is also to be the focus of something which comes *to* the whole from outside itself. Mission is a gift of Christ to a church: it is not a derivative of a church. Mission does not originate in a church, nor does a church possess a mission: it becomes mission by participating in Christ's Mission. An organization for mission should be a reminder to a church that participation in the Christ-event means participation in Christ's Mission, and that a church stands as recipient of Christ's gift of mission, and not as the origin or proprietor of it.

An organization for mission is not, then, simply a mouthpiece or instrument of a church: it also has the responsibility of speaking to a church in the name of Christ, in reminder, warning and correction of its understanding and practice of what this aspect of participation in the Christ-event means. It therefore has a ministry *to* a church as well as for it. It is also true that a church may have to remind an organization for mission of its true calling. As always in church life the relationship is one of mutual responsibility. In this an analogy may be seen with the Ministry of the Word and Sacraments, which is also a gift of Christ to a church, and not simply a derivative from a church.

If any organization for mission is to fulfil its duty to Christ and to the whole body, it is essential that its purpose and activities should be centred in this focal point of the proclamation of the name. That cannot, however, mean that it can be isolated from the other activities of the body of Christ's people. Any such isolation denies what we have seen to be the essential unity of the commitment of the whole person to Jesus Christ (see above, pp. 21 ff.) and so distorts both the mission and the other activities. Worship, cut off from the proclamation of the name to those who have not heard it, becomes introverted and precious—less the honouring of God's name than a display of liturgical erudition or artistic pyrotechnics. The service of our fellow men, if it is rendered in isolation from or forgetfulness of the proclamation of the name, is liable to become condescending, sentimental—"charity" in the corrupt sense of that once lovely word. (What is here in mind is the isolation of these activities from each other in the total activity of Christian congregations. It is not suggested that every act of service to our fellows must be accompanied by a proclamation of the name.) Christian nurture cut off from the proclamation of the name equips Christians only for living in the company of Christians, not for living in the world. And, equally, the proclamation of the name cut off from worship becomes aggressive, proud, individualistic, and forgets that it is the servant of Christ and not His proprietor; cut off from the service of our fellow men it becomes superior, abstract, disembodied, the purveying of propositions instead of the transmission of a life: cut off from Christian nurture it becomes thin, superficial, at worst a mere "scalp hunting", a drawing of men into a new compartment rather than their incorporation in a new living body. The aspects which we noted at the outset (pp. 21 ff.), as aspects of the total response of the whole personality to the Christ-event must be held together both in the life of the individual Christian and in the life of the local congregation.

The point at which these varied forms of Christian activity should be most fully seen as parts of one whole is in the local congregation. It is in the local congregation that Christians are most fully involved in them all as a whole, and where the one life which they manifest is most plain to be seen. Any forms of organization for wider purposes (including mission) which tend to split this oneness in worship, nurture, service and proclamation is to that extent condemned. For its full participation in and expression of the new life in Christ, the local congregation needs to hold them together.

We have directed this discussion principally to the situation of foreign mission organizations originating in the West in order to secure some degree of concreteness by limitation to one aspect of a very diverse scene. It is hoped, however, that it will be apparent that much that is here said is equally relevant to organizations for home missions. Christians in Asia are increasingly engaged in foreign mission. In so far as what is here said arises from a true understanding of the nature of mission, it may also have relevance for them as they concern themselves with questions of organization for mission. It is to be hoped that they will seek such forms of organization as express in their circumstances to-day an understanding of the meaning of participation in Christ's mission in the world, and will not be tempted to repeat patterns of organization which have arisen in other parts of the world in different historical circumstances, and which are clearly entering a period of radical revision. For all Christians everywhere need to remember that it is not mission organizations which determine what is mission: it is participation in Christ's Mission which determines what is mission, and it is that, in any given set of historical circumstances, which must determine the forms of our organizations.

Organization is important as a servant, and not as an end. Its chief importance as a servant is to make possible the service of persons, providing the framework within which personal service can be called forth, set free to serve, and nurtured and developed to its maximum capacity. To that function of an organization for mission we must now turn.

CHAPTER 12

MISSIONARIES

KNOWLEDGE OF THE CHRIST-EVENT IS PERSONALLY conveyed. One may know the facts about the historic person, Jesus of Nazareth, from a written record. But any knowledge of the Christ-event as the decisive event in history, still more any awareness of its critical, decisive meaning for my personal history, depends upon the testimony of persons. Each of us has received the Gospel in this sense from other persons: each of us is dependent on others for our hearing of this Word.

The clear recognition of and emphasis upon this personal communication of the Gospel was one of the strengths of foreign missions in the nineteenth century. They were primarily and distinctively concerned with the sending of persons to proclaim the name of the Redeemer where it was not known. In so doing they expressed an essential insight into the character of God's redemptive act, that it was done in a Person—indeed through *the* Person who is the ultimate standard for our understanding of the meaning of personal existence—and that it spoke to persons in the centre of their being as persons.

We may well see more clearly than a former era that a person is a person in community. We may be more aware that such personal testimony to Jesus Christ cannot be divorced from the life of the believing community, and is not fully effective without the witness to Him given by communities of persons living "in Christ". We may well recognize more fully that the telling of the name to persons is a focal point of, and not a substitute for, a wider witness in the structures of human societies. But if we forget or lose this conviction that the Gospel is personally conveyed, we shall have lost something which is central and essential to the Christian mission.

The basic form of this personal communication of the Gospel is that in which every Christian shares, in his speaking of Jesus Christ to those with whom he has continuing personal relationships. But to draw from this the conclusion, as is sometimes done, that "we are all missionaries now" is an unwarrantable over-simplification. It ignores the differentiation of gifts and functions within the body of which the New Testament speaks, and thereby destroys the possibility of particular callings of Christians to engage especially in one particular form of service. It ignores the fact that there are groups of people and areas of life in which the Christ-event will not be proclaimed unless some Christians are specially set aside and specially equipped to live amongst those groups or within those areas for the purpose of bearing witness within them to the Christ-event. The emphasis in the nineteenth century on foreign missions conceived as from Christendom to the non-Christian world may well have created a too restricting stereotype, which confined the title "missionary" to a full-time, paid, professional agent of a mission board, more especially one who worked outside his own country. Against such a limiting conception of the Christian mission, the current emphasis on "the apostolate of the laity" is a healthy reaction. But it is no necessary consequence of that realization of the wider scope of mission to deny either the need for those who are called and commissioned to give themselves specially and specifically to the proclamation of the name where it is not known or not acknowledged, or the legitimacy of such a call and commission.

That calling to special service in mission must, however, be rightly understood. It is a calling to service on behalf of the whole, not apart from the whole. In a way analogous to that which we have discussed in connection with an or-

ganization for mission, this must affect the relationships
and the nature of the work of a missionary. The relationships with the congregations who commission him or her
should be such as to help them to a sense of personal involvement in mission. Inasmuch as a missionary works in
a particular place and in specific tasks, such a relationship
with congregations can bring them a sense of involvement
that is concrete, actual, immediate as distinct from a
merely abstract and theoretical recognition of an obligation. Again, in the congregations in whose area the missionary works, the relationship must be such as to be a
focus of their participation in mission, not a substitute for
it. In both cases, it is through persons that Christ's Mission
in the world is realized not as an abstraction, an external-
ity, or an organization, but as an action in which I am
personally involved in the actual world.

To recognize the continued place in the Christian mission of those who are specially called and commissioned to
the service of mission is not, however, to justify the assumption that yesterday's understanding of the place and function of the missionary can continue unexamined into
to-morrow. Any understanding of the meaning of mission
in the new circumstances of our time is bound to have its
repercussions on the understanding of the rôle of the missionary. We may indicate one or two which arise from the
considerations advanced in this essay.

If mission is from the new age into the present age, then
there can be no justification for confining either the term
"missionary" or the use of missionaries to those who go
outside their own country. There have always been both
mission organizations and those who have served them as
missionaries who have been concerned with the Christian
mission in their own country. But in general usage, and
still more in the habits of thought of Christians, the words
"a missionary" have evoked first of all the picture of a
missionary in another land than his own. It seems time to
recognize frankly that Christ's Mission is one everywhere

in the world, and that "missionaries", in the sense of those called and commissioned to special service in mission, are needed in all lands.[1]

A second connotation of the words "a missionary" has been that he is a full-time agent of an organization for mission. The continuance of this conception into the future is questionable. The penetration of the areas of human living for the sake of mission which we have emphasized as an essential part of mission to-day will, in our view, call more and more for the service of Christians who enter them for the sake of articulating the Christ-event within them. Those who undertake this task will not only have to be fully trained in the particular type of activity concerned but, for the most part, to be fully involved in it. They cannot therefore be full-time agents of an organization for mission, in the sense of being wholly at the disposition of a mission organization. Yet if their basic calling is to the service of mission in these spheres, and if they are commissioned by a mission organization to enter them for the purpose of mission, they are in a real sense missionaries. To confine that term to those who are full-time agents of an organization for mission would be to fall into the error of making the organization the criterion of mission, and to allow "organization" to become master. Are not the calling to special service for mission and the commissioning by a body responsible for mission more appropriate criteria for the recognition of a missionary than whether or not he is a full-time agent of an organization for mission? To accept such criteria, it will be noted, is not to acquiesce in the contention that "we are all missionaries now", because they require a calling to special service for mission, entry into a sphere of work for the sake of mission, and the recognition of both of these by a body responsible for mission.

Missionaries engaged in this type of service within the structures of human society, which may obviously be in their own country or abroad, would also be "the part on behalf of the whole". It would be part of their task to serve as points of concentration for other Christians engaged in the same sphere of human activity and to provide the help and support and guidance which we saw to be necessary when we were discussing the Christian mission in the spheres of education or national politics and government. They would be in a position to give such help because they would be fully involved in the particular sphere of activity, and so could speak from inside it; at the same time they would have received training as missionaries, which would naturally include the study of the Bible and the Christian faith and the practice of the devotional life now included in missionary training courses. What other training would be appropriate to their sphere of missionary action presents an exciting sphere for thought and experiment; their presence in a missionary training college might lead to some stimulating innovations in courses on "missionary methods" and "communicating the Gospel", as well as some illuminating additions to courses on cultures and religions.

This suggests that, in the future, organizations for mission may have to be ready for a much more diversified and flexible type of activity. So far as foreign missions are concerned, we have envisaged them becoming less the channel for all types of Christian activity, and concentrating increasingly on the core of mission. This would mean that fewer missionaries would be engaged in activities within the structure and under the control of a church or mission. Missionaries as such would be increasingly those who were dispersed in the "secular" life of the structures of human society.[2] A comparable development would be expected in regard to "home" missions. This would mean that organizations for mission could not expect to direct the work of all missionaries in the same way as they have done in the past. They would have to be prepared to send many of them "into the world" rather than expect to be able to keep them within the orbit of church work and church or mission institutions. Their Christian "base" would be in the local church in the place where their work took them, not in the mission organization, and their Christian colleagues would be those Christians who were engaged in the same sphere of activity.

The result of such concentration on the core of mission might well be a reduction in the number of foreign missionaries—which is not to say that the number of Christians going from their own countries to serve the Christian churches in other countries would necessarily diminish, for those who went for purposes other than the special service of mission would go through other channels. Any who measure faithfulness or effectiveness in mission by statistics would no doubt recoil from such a prospect. Provided, however, that the reduction in the number of foreign missionaries was for the right reasons, it might well benefit the work of the Christian mission as a whole. If it meant that those who went abroad as missionaries were really engaged in being points of concentration for mission, that would have two beneficial results. It would bring into sharp focus again the central purpose of mission, to proclaim the name of the Redeemer where it is not known or not acknowledged; and it would underline the fact that mission is not the responsibility only of those who are agents of an organization for mission, but of all Christians. There are at least some places in the world where mission staffs are so numerous that it must be extremely difficult for the local Christians to feel that any need or responsibility for mission rests on them. There are many more where involvement in duties within the Christian community leaves missionaries little opportunity to be points of concentration in mission. So long as organizations for mission are regarded as the bearers of the total mission, rather than as points of concentration on behalf of the whole, neither situation is likely to be remedied.

The number of those qualified to undertake the work of a missionary as here envisaged may be comparatively small. The Christian who feels called to serve in a country where Christian manpower is more urgently needed than in his own, but who feels no call to special service in mission, will rightly find the channel for his service through some other channel than an organization for mission. Those who are called to special service in mission in some sphere of activity in society—education, industry and so forth—will need to have qualifications enabling them to render full and effective service to society in that sphere, and in addition, training as a missionary; not all such may find a suitable professional opening abroad. Many of those posts within the service of a church which the church desires to have filled from stronger churches abroad will be handled through other agencies than an organization for mission. The number of posts within a church which are points of concentration for mission and are therefore rightly the responsibility of an organization for mission may be comparatively small, and of these, some are likely to require persons with special equipment, e.g. to serve on the staff of a lay training institute designed to help Christians in the discharge of their responsibility in society, or to be a member of a team of workers engaged in evangelism in a new urban area, or in rural community development in an area without any congregation, and to contribute some special knowledge or experience to such enterprises.

The concentration of the foreign mission on its task of being a focus for mission on behalf of the whole has in view two aims. Part of its aim would be to evoke a greater and fuller realization and practice of the apostolate of the laity. An essential function of the missionary would be to emphasize the responsibility of all Christians to participate in mission, to help them to discover what that meant in practical terms in their own particular situations, and to assist in providing them with whatever training they needed to carry it out. And, secondly, the more it was made clear that the mission is one mission everywhere in the world, that everywhere it is from the age to come into this present age, and that the foreign mission is there not to carry out the total mission instead of the local Christians, but to help in providing points of concentration through which the local Christians also are better able to realize and discharge their responsibility in mission, the more likelihood there is that the foreign missionaries will be joined by home missionaries, equally called to special service in mission, commissioned to it by the appropriate body in their own church, sharing fully and equally with the foreign missionaries in being points of concentration for mission in their own country.

The more we have considered the implications of these two leading thoughts, that the Gospel is personally conveyed and that mission organizations are "the part on behalf of the whole", the more they have brought again into the foreground a thought which has been in mind for many years, that what is needed is something like an "order" of missionaries. (The term may not be a very happy one, and may be liable to misunderstanding, but it is difficult to discover a better.) An order of those committed to personal service in the proclamation of the name, and commissioned to that task explicitly on behalf of the whole body, would hold together those two basic conceptions. It would, moreover, conserve, in a form adaptable to contemporary needs in mission, two other values which have marked the foreign missionary movement in the past two centuries. The first is the unreserved and complete commitment of a person's life in the service of mission, including the readiness to leave one's own home and make one's home in an entirely strange environment for the sake of mission. The second is the strength and purposiveness which characterize a community bound by a common loyalty and committed to a specific common purpose.

It is possible to envisage the outlines of such an order. It would avoid all pretension to being the total mission: it would be quite deliberately the servant of the mission, with the explicit intention of providing points of concentration for mission wherever they were needed. It would avoid becoming a self-sufficient or self-contained entity: its members would be at the disposal of the Christian community (but only for mission) wherever they were called to serve. It would require of those who joined it a clear and definite calling to special service in the focal point of mission, the proclamation of the name where it has not been heard or is not acknowledged, and a willingness to be committed to that task without reservation, to receive whatever training the task required and to go into any geographical area or area of human living to serve wherever there was a need in mission which they could fulfil. Its requirement for admission would therefore be primarily commitment to mission, and secondarily willingness to be sent anywhere in the service of mission, whether in one's own country or outside it. It would thus point to both the primary and secondary forms of being sent (see above, chap. 2). The basic requirement of commitment to mission points to mission as fundamentally from the new age into the present age. The secondary requirement of willingness to be sent anywhere in mission points to the secondary form of sentness—"to the ends of the earth", beyond as well as within one's one culture, and by and on behalf of the whole people of God. Thus at any one time some of its members would be serving in their own country and others in other countries.

Ideally, its membership would be international, to make clear that it was the servant of the new humanity in Christ, and not of any national culture or way of life; but if that were achieved, it would need centres in each country from which its members were drawn and to which they would return if they were serving abroad, to make clear that to be a servant of the new humanity is not to abandon one's present humanity with its roots in one's own country and culture, but to bring the distinctive gifts of that country and culture to the obedience and service of a new whole, a redeemed manhood. Its members would be expected to find their spiritual home and nurture in the local church in the place in which they were at work: but they would also have some simple common rule designed to sustain their sense of special calling to mission, and, because it was a common rule, to be a means of preserving their sense of belonging to a distinctive community with a special calling. On occasion, members in any area would meet together for worship, Bible study, and prayer, and to share experience and insights.

The members of the order would be engaged in a variety of spheres of work, some in the mission-to-man-in-society and so employed in industry, education, politics and government and so on, and deriving their livelihood therefrom, and some in the direct service of churches, in lay training centres, in evangelistic work, in other aspects of the churches' life where they were reaching out beyond the churches' own borders into the total life of the community. The order would thus both provide a medium whereby separated areas of human living could be brought into contact with each other within the context of commitment to Jesus Christ in whom it is God's purpose to sum up all things, and would enable those engaged in mission in different spheres to see the unity of their task and to learn from one another's experience. It would provide a sense of "togetherness" which was formerly given by a group of missionaries working in one area and within one organization, which, without such an order, might be lost in the future, when missionaries to fulfil their calling must be dispersed through a variety of different occupations and be working under many different auspices.

Such a conception is not new. Attention has often been drawn to the analogies between missionary societies in the nineteenth century and the monastic movements of earlier centuries. The idea of the "non-professional missionary", engaged in "secular" employment but with a missionary purpose, has been under discussion for many years. But although the conception of an "order" of missionaries is not new, stated thus as one means whereby the meaning of mission to-day may be expressed, it will doubtless be regarded as absurdly idealistic. And of course this is an idealized picture. We have spoken, for instance, of "an order" in the singular, as though there could be one order serving the whole people of Christ as a focus for mission in the world. But since the people of Christ is divided, a living relationship would in practice, no doubt, only be possible if there were several such orders each related to some actual part of this divided people. This need not imply a mere acceptance of present denominational frontiers. Some denominations are close enough in basic convictions and churchmanship to enable such an order to be rooted in them together without loss of the sense of personal involvement which such an order would aim to provide.

It would be necessary to take care that any such orders were so arranged as to preserve the sense of a community bound together by a common purpose, which implies a real degree of local responsibility; any elaborate international organization would destroy its essential ethos, and transform its members from being points of concentration for mission into being some kind of international ecclesiastical diplomatic service. Nevertheless it should be possible by careful experiment and gradual growth to discover ways in which such orders could be genuinely rooted in the church life and in the cultures and countries of their members and yet realize, to some degree at least, a sense of being part of a common order in the service of the whole people of Christ. The rule of each order might include a common prayer for daily use. Their members could take care always to act on behalf of the whole body and not in the interests of only one part. Their local meetings might on occasion include members from all the orders in the area, irrespective of denomination. As opportunity and need offered, an order might send some of its members to work under the auspices of other denominations. In short, such orders, if they genuinely had a sense of also being part of one common order in the service of the mission of the new humanity in Christ, would find ways of being one more bond between the divided parts of Christ's people: and that is surely integral to the task of proclaiming the name of the one Redeemer of mankind.

It is tempting to try to draw out from all this the dimly seen outlines of the pattern of operation of the Christian mission of to-morrow. The outline which begins to emerge is something like this. In each country the churches have their organization for mission—board or committee or what you will. It is organically related, by whatever means are locally appropriate, to the life of the church both in its local congregation and its central courts. It serves as a centre of information and experience gained in mission and makes that information and experience available to all parts of the church's life and work. It calls forth those who have a calling to special service in mission, arranges for their training, and for their commissioning by the church, and appoints them within a missionary order to service at home or abroad. It does not expect to control or direct the work of those it appoints. They will be in the service either of a secular employer or of a church body: in the latter case the organization for mission may or may not, according to circumstances, provide the financial support needed. It receives from churches abroad those whom they have commissioned to special service in mission (but not those sent from abroad for other forms of service) and in consultation with the sending church arranges for their work, if it is under church auspices; in any case it seeks to link them with those engaged in mission from within its own country. In all its planning it keeps in close touch with comparable bodies in other churches in the country, and common plans are worked out and operated for the use of available resources of people and money in any given area, so that the mission in that area is planned as one operation and the points of greatest need and opportunity receive maximum help from all sources.

The missionaries, whether from that country or abroad,

seek to be focal points for the mission of the Christian community as a whole, some by gathering the Christians in one area engaged in one profession or occupation to think and pray together about the articulation of the Christ-event within that profession and occupation, some by being the focus of a team which seeks to gather new congregations in areas where there are none. On occasion, these two aspects are combined in a total approach to the community in a given area over the whole range of its life. It becomes part of the task of the organization for mission to be a focal point of these and other diverse operations and to keep them in touch with other aspects of the churches' work; thus there may be revealed a need for some particular type of literature, which is either referred to the church's literature committee or to a "secular" publisher, perhaps through a missionary at work in the publishing trade; or the mission in one industry in one area may show that representations need to be made to a local government authority, say on housing, which is handled through the church's department of social responsibility. In such ways it keeps the whole church conscious of the missionary dimension of its existence. . . .

Yes, it is tempting thus to try to see the outlines of mission to-morrow. Of course, it is wildly Utopian? In one sense of course it is; it is a long, long way removed from the actualities of the contemporary scene. Yet if we are ever to move in action, and not merely in words, beyond the present forms of organization, which are widely agreed to require considerable modification if they are to be effective for the task of mission to-day, we need some such picture of the new forms in which mission should express itself.

Such a picture should arise from the effort to "think together" the meaning of mission as given in the Christ-event and the situation of Christians in the present world. The picture which we have given as a result of attempting to do this may well be the wrong one, because we have not rightly understood either the meaning of mission given in the Christ-event or the actualities of the contemporary scene, or both. Then let it be replaced by a more adequate one. But do not let us delude ourselves with the notion that participation in Christ's Mission to-day is possible without changes in existing habits of thought and organization —changes which, when first envisaged, will seem wildly Utopian, and which will certainly not be painless in operation.

The organizations for mission which have grown up during the past century and a half have indeed received a great trust—the trust of being "remembrancers" to the whole body of Christians of their calling to proclaim the name of the Redeemer to "the uttermost part of the earth". They are rightly concerned to ensure that that trust is faithfully discharged. But they would conceive the requirements of faithfulness wrongly if they were to suppose that the trust can only be discharged if the range of activities, the forms of organization and the pattern of relationships which at present exist are preserved unchanged. That would be to confuse the abiding commitment with the historically conditioned, contingent forms of expression of it. "Mission" must not be identified without qualification with organizations for mission, nor must a critical scrutiny of the latter be regarded as necessarily a threat to the former.

The deeper the understanding of and commitment to Mission, the greater the freedom to change the pattern of organization for mission. Obedience to the calling to share in Christ's Mission involves finding the right forms to express that obedience in the circumstances of to-day. We must indeed learn from our past. Not to do so would be to repudiate what God the Holy Spirit has done in it. But we learn from it not in order to be in bondage to it, but to respond, in the freedom which is Christ's gift, to the claims of present obedience upon us, our activities, our organizations, our relationships, that God the Holy Spirit may have His way with us.

CHAPTER 13

SOME QUESTIONS TO CHURCHES

W E HAVE SEEN THAT THE CHRISTIAN MISSION IN THE
world arises from the Christ-event, and is the Christian mission to the extent that it participates in Christ's
Mission. The Church, in the sense of the whole company
of those who acknowledge the Christ-event and are drawn
into it, arises from the same source. The understanding of
mission as participation in Christ's Mission has therefore
something to say to our understanding of the Church. And
since the Church has its empirical manifestation in the
churches, in the sense of ecclesiastical organizations existing in this historical aeon, it is reasonable to suppose that
this understanding of mission may put some questions to
them about their life as the Church. It should be noted,
however, that these questions arise from mission as participation in Christ's Mission, not from missions as such:
missions, in the sense of organizations for mission, are (as
we have seen in the preceding chapters) themselves also
questioned by Mission.

It seems to us that it is urgent that churches should take
seriously the questions put to them by mission. Much of
the thinking of the past about the Church on which our
present ecclesiologies are based and which determines our
habits of mind and the lines along which our discussions
proceed, has been carried on in what might be called the
"Christendom context", i.e. in a context where Christianity was in some sense the "official" religion and where
the whole community was regarded as in some sense
Christian. This seems broadly true of all ecclesiological

thinking in the post-Constantinian era, including the debates about the nature of the Church at the time of the Reformation. Arising in that context, thought about the Church has not been sufficiently aware of the setting of the Church's life in human society in rebellion against God and informed by other faiths and loyalties. It has not felt with sufficient acuteness one essential dimension of the life of the Church in the world, that it lives always and in every situation in a missionary setting. It has lacked the sense of the "foreignness" of the Church. On the other hand, because of the historical circumstances in which they arose, many missions in the modern era have remained, until comparatively recently, to a large extent isolated from the places where thinking about the Church was carried on. Their experience has contributed less than it ought to have done to that thinking, and they have drawn on it less than they ought to have done for the illumination of their tasks. This isolation of thought and experience between churches and missions happily has for some time past rapidly been breaking down. But habits of thought built up over centuries are not quickly altered, and it remains true that a great deal of our way of thinking about the Church is inadequate to handle a situation in which the churches find themselves everywhere in a missionary situation, for which categories derived from a "Christendom" situation are almost entirely irrelevant.

The rethinking of our ecclesiologies in the light of the understanding that participation in the Christ-event means participation in Christ's Mission in the world is a task which will require a couple of generations or so. In the meantime, actual decisions have to be made about church affairs and about the work of missions which cannot wait for fully re-formulated ecclesiologies. Moreover, the most creative thought about the Church (as about any other aspect of Christian faith and life) does not take place in abstraction from the pressures of such concrete decisions, but from within them. What is important in this situation is not that we should know all the answers to the ecclesiological questions, but that we should be ready to acknowledge that we do not. Freedom from the imprisonment of habitual thinking, awareness of fresh horizons, readiness to carry on our thinking in new and unfamiliar contexts, openness to fresh thought and fresh experience which do not fit into our accustomed categories—these are more important at the moment than any detailed, fully formulated and entirely coherent system of thought about the nature of the Church. It may therefore be worth while to try to discover some of the more basic questions to the churches which arise from the understanding of mission which the preceding chapters have attempted to outline.

Those questions seem to be in principle two, one concerned mainly with the churches' understanding of themselves and the other with their understanding of their relation with human societies.

Mission has been understood in this essay as action which takes place between two focal points: it is the proclamation of the Christ-event as an event which happened in history from beyond history, and it is witness to God's purpose, made known in that event, to sum up all things in Christ. It is the attempt to articulate the Christ-event in any given set of historical circumstances. To make that attempt, from within the forms of time and space in which it lives, mission must necessarily point backwards to the historic event and forwards to its full consummation. In so doing it is really pointing beyond the historical era, not in any idealistic way which would make history unreal, but in the way of saying that the reality of any particular set of circumstances in history is made known by the articulation of the Christ-event within them. It therefore has to recognize that its attempt to articulate the Christ-event at any given point in time and space is never final or complete: it is always contingent and partial: yet it is never just contingent and partial, because what it seeks to articulate is that which is final and complete. Mission points

179

away from itself to Christ: but it points to Christ, known in the historical event, anticipated in the consummation, from within the here and now of particular and actual circumstances.

Now, if the Church is constituted by the Christ-event, and if one dimension of its life is given by participation in Christ's Mission, that understanding of mission has something to say to the understanding of the form of the life of the Church within this historical era. In any given set of historical circumstances, a church's articulation of the Christ-event can never claim to be final and complete. If it were, it would be removed outside history and would have no existence in the contingent circumstances of that particular time and place. This consideration puts a question mark against any claims for finality and completeness on behalf of any actual form of church order. A church order may be the best and fullest articulation of the Christ-event in the given circumstances; it does not thereby escape the contingencies and relativities necessarily involved in being an articulation *at that time and place*. On the other hand, this consideration equally puts a question mark against all views which would regard all forms of church order as either institutional obstacles to a living obedience to Christ in the "secular" world, ("Let's abandon the churches, and go out and be Christians in the world!") or as merely temporary and so to say *ad hoc* arrangements to enable Christians to meet and act together in any particular time and place. For it is the Christ-event which is to be articulated in church order, and that event happened in history and so has a historical and specific character which must be recognizable in any articulation of it.

Perhaps this is no more than one way of stating the dilemma which has haunted discussion of church order down the centuries, namely, in the attempt to express in the structure of a corporate body an event which is both in history and the "end" of history, what is the proper relation of historical continuity and of the possibility of change in the light of changing historical circumstances? It is, however, possible that to view that dilemma in the more dynamic context of the missionary situation of the churches, instead of in the more static one of a "Christendom" situation, may throw some fresh light on its solution, at least for our times. For example, consideration of questions of church order in the context of the missionary situation makes largely irrelevant what might be called the archaeological form of the discussion. The debate about whether a particular form of church order can be shown to be historically continuous with that in the New Testament has not only run into an impasse in terms of the historical evidence: it is also largely irrelevant to a church in a missionary situation. For in that situation the question which arises is not, "Can this church order be shown, by historical evidence, to be historically continuous with the church order of the New Testament?" The question which arises in that situation is, "Is this church order articulating the Christ-event in this particular time and place?" Continuity in terms of an institution with a continuous existence in history is no guarantee that it is, for that kind of continuity ignores the elements of change and contingency in the historical era. But neither will it do to pretend that there is no historical element in church order, for in fact the Christ-event happened in history.

The continuity to be sought, however, lies not in an institution with a continuous historical existence, but in the Christ-event itself. The kind of questions about a church order which from this missionary situation it would seem to be necessary to ask are: "Is this church order such as to bear constant and unequivocal testimony to what God has done in Christ? Does it provide the means whereby its members are constantly involved afresh in that event, renewed in their awareness of their new humanity in Christ, and sustained in their living from out of that new humanity within the life of a society still governed by 'the rulers of the darkness of this world'? Does it point them forward to

Christ as Him in whom it is God's purpose to sum up all things?"

Obviously, such questions cannot be answered without reference to such familiar elements in discussion of church order as the place of the Bible in the life of a church, the meaning and ordering of worship, preaching and the sacraments, the discipline of the life of a church and its members and the relation within that discipline of faith and ethics, and so on. But there is at least the possibility that, considered in this context, some fresh understanding of these elements of church order may be given to us. If there is a particular contribution which may be made from the standpoint of mission to that fresh understanding, it is perhaps that pointed to in the last of the above questions. It is from the dimension of mission that a church should be kept aware of the goal of God's purpose to sum up all things in Christ, and so should be reminded that its church order must point not only to the Christ-event in history, but also to the Christ-event at the end of history.

Perhaps this affects the substance rather than the form of a church order—the content of the sermons rather than the fact of preaching, the content of prayers and hymns rather than the fact of a liturgy, the teaching given about and in church discipline rather than the fact of a disciplined structure of church life. But whether in form or content or both, from the standpoint of mission sharing in church life should constantly point Christians to the purpose of God to sum up all things in Christ. It should not be possible, as it sometimes seems at present possible, to participate in church life as a means of escape from the pressures of contemporary society, or of securing one's private salvation in a realm which is completely detached from and so largely irrelevant to the so-called "secular" world. It should not be possible to misunderstand the Church as an end in itself: it should be unmistakably clear that the Church is the "part for the whole" of humanity, that it is the means whereby God through the Christ-event is gathering all things into their head in Jesus Christ, that it must hold before men the goal to which this created world, in all its variety and in all forms of its life, moves.

This leads us inevitably to the second question, which arises from our understanding of mission: the question of the churches' understanding of their relation with human societies. We have suggested that one consequence of our understanding of mission is that Christians need to have a relationship of "involved detachment" with the societies in which they live; they need to hold together both their solidarity with human society and their separation from it. If that is a requirement of participation in Christ's Mission, it is also required of the churches.

Is this, in fact, how the churches regard their relation with the societies in which they are set? And do their organizational arrangements and practices in fact reflect such a relationship? The answers to these questions are not to be given from outside any particular church: from outside, it is not possible fully to understand the realities of any actual church situation. But the questions may be suggested from outside without impertinence and perhaps helpfully, since within the situation it may not always be seen that there are questions to be answered. In some church situations the question may be: "Are we thinking of ourselves as and behaving as though we were simply the community at its religious exercises? If so, are we sharing in Christ's Mission?" This question does not arise only in church situations where the historical situation is one of an established church. It arises wherever the church reflects the prevailing ethos of the community and applies no critical judgment to it: and there are churches of this type in all the continents.

On the other hand, the question in some church situations is: "Are we thinking of ourselves as and behaving as though we were just a religious club with no real responsibility for the life of the community in which we are set?" This question does not arise only in situations of "free" churches, or churches which have no formal relationships with the structures of the community. Established churches, or churches which have historic connections with the community, may have defences in their structures or practice against such irresponsibility: but their real life as churches, and especially the life of their members, may be lived within their church structures in a way which disregards the responsibility for the community to which those structures point. And all churches need to ask themselves whether changes in the structures of the societies around them have not passed them by, so that whatever means they once may have had of maintaining a creative relationship with the corporate life of those communities have become largely mere archaisms, with little living content.

Such questions arise primarily and rightly in terms of a church's relationship with the community in which it is set. Yet, in the context of participation in Christ's Mission in the world, they cannot be answered from within that relationship. For a church in one country is "the part for the whole": it is a representative of the whole company of Christ's people, the whole of which is "sent" into the world. So churches must ask themselves also whether they are rightly expressing within their own community their participation in world mission. Are they in their life and work in that community forgetting their world-wide Christian links, or making those links merely secondary and ancillary to their local life? If they are, can they really be expressing the life of the new humanity in Christ—or are they merely giving a pseudo-Christian cloak to the life of their local community? (One test of this arises when a crucial issue of national policy in the international scene arises: is a church's judgment then determined by awareness of responsibility to the world-wide Christian community or is it determined by "the national interest?") How far is the judgment of the world-wide Christian community considered in relation to the church's witness and service in the local community, or does the church consider

184

itself self-sufficient, and in no need of the stimulus and correction of the wider Christian community?

The pointedness and practicality of the questions arising from the missionary dimension of a church's life may be illustrated in relation to one point, namely, the local unit of church life—a pertinent instance in view of what was said earlier about the significance of the local congregation as the centre in which the different aspects of Christian life come together into a whole. In England, there have been, broadly speaking, two conceptions of the local unit of church life: the parish and the gathered congregation. Each has its connections with a conception of the relation of the church to the community, the former with a conception of the church as including all the members of the community, the latter with a conception of the church as gathering believers from out of the community. Each also reflects to some extent the era in which it arose. The parish unit has natural affinities with a predominantly agricultural society, with clearly defined local social units and a comparatively stationary population. The gathered congregation has natural affinities with a mercantile community, in which small towns assume importance but where the urban unit is not too large for a cross-section of its life to be represented in one congregation. Each tends to express a certain ethos of church life and to influence the practice of church life as well as the habits of thought about the church. But to-day, English society is highly industrialized, more and more shaped by the application of technology, with an increasingly mobile population. The once coherent social units of village or town are being split up, so that relationships within the social structures are based less and less on geography and more and more on occupation and interest.

In that changed situation it is tempting to say that both units of church life, the parish and the gathered congregation, are outmoded and irrelevant and ought to give place to a new form of unit. In one sense this is true, and to cling

185

to a traditional form of church organization just because it is traditional is to risk "making void the word of God by your tradition".[1] But in another sense it is too sweeping. These units of church life each express something of the Christ-event. They are not solely the products of a particular social structure; they are products of attempts to articulate the Christ-event within a particular social structure. The parish unit expresses, for example, the responsibility of Christians towards their geographical neighbours; and since the Christian mission bids us take geography seriously, that responsibility is not one to be excluded from a church's organization. Because we live in a technological age it does not follow that Christians are called upon to acquiesce in the disruption of the local geographical community which is so often (though perhaps not necessarily) one of its consequences. On the contrary, their witness to man in society may well have to include a witness to the significance of the local geographical community as a necessary element in the structure of any society in which men are to be fully human. Again, the parish unit expresses the responsibility of a church for the total life of the community in which it is set. Wisely understood and used, it can remind a church that it exists not for itself but for humanity, and it can provide the framework for a series of creative relationships with different aspects of the life of society.

The gathered congregation at this point expresses the other aspect of the truth, that the church is not only involved in society but must also be detached from it. It calls attention to the fact that the Christ-event comes into history from outside it. It, therefore, supplies a point of criticism of the community's standards and practices from outside it. Furthermore, by its emphasis on personal Christian faith as a condition of membership and on the importance of the responsibility of all the members to strive to keep the life of the congregation as a whole open and obedient to Christ, it points to the corporate nature of the new manhood in Christ. Wisely used and understood, it can be a witness to the fact that those who are taken into the Christ-event are indeed a new "nation, a people for God's own possession".[2] Because we live in a technological age, it does not follow that Christians must acquiesce in the pressures within it towards conformity, standardization, mass values. On the contrary, their witness to man in society may well have to include the visible affirmation of loyalty to standards which are not derived from that society, and commitment to a fellowship whose origin is not within similar interests or occupations or outlook, but in an event which is unique and which creates a fellowship which rejoices in its diversity.

It is too simple, then, simply to abandon these units of local church life and seek something entirely new. To do so would be almost certainly to create a unit which was either a mere reflection of the spirit of the age, and so incapable of witness to an event outside that age, or one which was so idealistically remote from contemporary actualities as to be irrelevant to life as it is actually lived. At the same time it is abundantly clear that neither the parish nor the gathered congregation is a unit of local church life which is capable, by itself and in its present form, of carrying the Christian mission, much less of expressing the totality of the Christian life in any locality in the circumstances of our day.

Is not what is required, then, that first we should recognize and bring together those expressions of the Christ-event which have been conserved in the parish unit and in the gathered congregation unit, and so far as possible ensure that they find expression through the life of all the congregations in whatever vestigial geographical communities may be left to us? (Local Councils of Churches have a strategic role to play here.) Next, that we should look for those places in the life of the community which are clearly left outside the present structure of church life, and ask ourselves what new form of church unit is needed to articulate the Christ-event within them. A good deal of hopeful experiment is, of course, taking place along these lines already—house churches, industrial missions, "frontier" type groups, "guild" churches and so on. A further question which arises in this connection is whether our churches are providing the nurture which their members need if they are to sustain their Christian life and witness in society. The parish church and the gathered congregation both did so in the past. It may be that we have suitable instruments in our church structures for doing so today, but it is not obvious that we have, or that if we have, we are using them. Thirdly, that we should reflect on the results of these two processes to see what we should learn from them about the nature of the Church and what modifications they call for in the constitutions and organizational structures of our churches, so that those institutions and organizational structures may bear a fuller and more adequate witness to the Christ-event in the context of this particular place and time.

This instance of the kind of question which our understanding of mission puts to churches concerning their relation with human societies has been treated at some length because it illustrates several aspects of the point we are making. First, it is involvement in mission which raises the question. So long as we are not concerned with the proclamation of the name to men and to men in society, the traditional units of church life may not appear to us inadequate or outmoded. We may deplore the fact that the advent of the motor-car has depleted the congregation, but we are not likely to probe the matter further and try to find out where the motor-car is in fact taking those who might once have been in the congregation, and what it is in fact doing to the structure of the society to which the congregation was in former days related. It is when we are concerned that men should know the name of their Redeemer *where they are*, that we begin to probe into the relation between the places where that name is proclaimed and the places where men in fact are.

Secondly, the organized structure of a church cannot remain unchanged without becoming an obstacle to, instead of an instrument of, the Christian mission. Loyalty to a traditional form of church structure is not sufficient to ensure the proclamation of Jesus Christ. We cannot live out of yesterday's obediences: we must find our own. Thirdly, we shall not discover our own by ignoring yesterday's, but by distinguishing in yesterday's forms those elements which are pointing to the Christ-event and those which were the reflection of the temporary and contingent elements in their circumstances, and so learning from them what must be included in our obedience, along with whatever new elements may be shown to us as required by our obedience in our own time.

This, in short, is the question which the mission puts to the churches: "Is your life turned inwards on yourself or outwards on the world?" If it is turned inwards, radical questions about the nature of the Church, about the practice of the churches, about their relation with human society, will not arise. Such questions arise from the attempt to articulate the Christ-event in the midst of the actualities of a given concrete set of historical circumstances. It is when that attempt is made that a church begins to understand the relativity and ambiguity of all its past attempts at such articulation, because it begins to see that they are not in fact testifying to the Christ-event in the circumstances of to-day. It is therefore saved from the error of identifying itself with the Kingdom of God and absolutizing its life or its claims on men. It is ready to have its life and structure brought under the judgment of Jesus Christ.

By the same token, it is in the attempt to articulate the Christ-event in a given set of historical circumstances that a church discovers by what it really lives: not by its continuity as a historical institution, nor by its relevance to present circumstances: not by its numerical strength, nor by its social or political influence: not indeed by anything which can be predicated of a church considered as a socio-logical entity among other such entities: but solely by its being constantly drawn into the Christ-event, and thereby being given a constantly renewed life. A church also needs to have proclaimed within it the name of its Redeemer: it is by the ever-renewed gift of His life that it lives.

So living, it knows that its real life is not finally at the mercy of historical contingency: it is at the mercy of God in Christ. In trust in His mercy it knows its real life taken up through the Christ-event into the whole doxology of heaven. And though its notes be broken and out of tune, it can yet join here and now in the anthem of heaven:

"Worthy is the Lamb that hath been slain to receive the power and riches and wisdom and might and honour and glory and blessing."[3]

CONCLUSION

MISSION AS DOXOLOGY

THE CHRISTIAN MISSION TAKES PLACE IN "THE LAST hour" between the Resurrection of Christ and the open manifestation of His reign. Here and now, in this place, in this moment, in these concrete circumstances, to articulate the Christ-event, to proclaim the name of the Redeemer, is to enthrone the Son of Man who is Lord of all and in whose pierced hands all things are gathered up and given back again to God the Father.

We have tried in these pages to speak to the actual, present circumstances of the activities of Christians in mission in the contemporary world, for it is in those actual, present circumstances that we are called to participate in Christ's Mission. His call to mission comes to us where we are. We respond from where we are or we do not respond at all.

Yet we misunderstand the calling to share in Christ's Mission if our attention is concentrated solely on our temporal circumstances, and if our question is only: "What is the next thing to do?" For the next thing to do in participation in Christ's Mission is only discerned if we set mission in the here and now in the context of its ultimate purpose, if we see it in its rightful setting in "the last hour".

The conclusion of Christ's Mission is His ascension. In His incarnation, His ministry on earth, His suffering and crucifixion He accomplished His work which God the Father had given Him, and in His resurrection God crowned that work with victory. So Christ "ascends" to God, is "exalted" to the right hand of God, the first fruits of a redeemed humanity and of the fulfilment of God's purpose in creation. The work is accomplished: it is offered to God: it is accepted. The deliverance of mankind into the life of God's reign is achieved. But this accomplished deliverance remains veiled, hidden save to faith.

It is to this complete work of Christ that the mission of Christians testifies. Wherever and whenever it is declared in word and deed, there is the disclosure of God's reign, full of the judgment and mercy of the living God in Christ.

Of course in the historical aeon in which we are set we must speak also of Christ's coming again. The historical aeon continues, extended in time and space, and the exalted Christ is veiled, known only to faith. From within the setting of time, we look for His coming at the end of this temporal sequence, that His exaltation may be open and manifest. But this is no new hour; this last hour is already upon us. And this is no new Christ, but Jesus of Nazareth.

This Event which in our temporal sequence we separate into its parts of incarnation, ministry, crucifixion, resurrection, ascension and final triumph is one Event, the divine "moment" of redemption and re-creation. It is therefore the moment also of judgment, of discrimination. By their response to it within the particular moment of time in which it comes to them, men decide for or against Christ, to accept or reject His Kingdom, to receive or refuse the life of the age to come. This is expressed most clearly, perhaps, in the Fourth Gospel, where Christ's freely accepted death is presented both as His glorification and as the judgment of men: but it is implicit in the whole New Testament pattern of obedience—death—risen life manifest in Jesus Christ and therefore the pattern of life for those who are incorporate in Him.

Mission is thus the articulation of the total event in this "last hour" which, in the temporal perspective of our historical aeon, is seen as the last hour between His coming and His coming again. The articulation of the total Event is both the bringing of men under judgment and the gathering of the people of God into Christ, that He may bring them in His exaltation to God the Father.

Seen in the perspective of this historical era, the Mission of Christ is a being sent into the life of mankind to break the bonds of its rebellion and open to it entry into the new life. Seen in the perspective of the "last hour", the Mission of Christ is the establishment of the centre of the new humanity to which come God's people from the ends of the earth to worship. These are not two processes, but one: the sending is also the gathering. The one stresses the aspect of witness among men, the other God's use of that witness in the fulfilment of His purpose to gather His people into Christ.

This is the fulfilment of the vision of the Old Testament of the gathering of God's people in "the last hour" from amongst all peoples to the true centre of worship (and there-fore of living).[1] In the Old Testament vision of the consum-mation of God's purpose, mankind is seen as waiting ex-pectantly for the manifestation of God's glory. God calls those who have survived the judgment of the "last hour"—a call which His people Israel echoes. The nations travel on the highway of God to Jerusalem, bringing their gifts, that they may worship at the house of prayer for all nations and share in the messianic banquet upon the mountain of God. In the New Testament, this vision of the Old Testament is presented as fulfilled in the Event of Jesus Christ. At His birth, the angels proclaim God's sum-mons to gather. Jesus is shown as the shepherd who is gathering the nations as a shepherd gathers his scattered flock. In this hour of fulfilment, men come from all nations to share the messianic feast, and to worship in the new Temple of His body in the new Jerusalem which is above, of which He is king.

But this is fulfilment, not merely extension of the Old Testament vision, fulfilment by transformation as well as completion. For the act of gathering is through the death

N*   195

of the king, and that death is at the same moment His glorification. The gathering is to the true centre of humanity, the New Man, Christ Jesus: but it is a gathering by a life poured out and so made available to all people, from within them and not only as external to them. So the command to go into all the world comes *after* His resurrection, when the risen life of the New Man is available to all through the completed act of redemption which ushers in the "last hour". And the commission to go out is given from the true centre of worship, and is itself in the form of a hymn of enthronement of the world's king who alone is worthy of worship.[2] So the going out is a part of the gathering to the centre, and is also part of the offering of adoration from all nations to the one God.

This gathering of the peoples is God's act in Jesus Christ. It is not something that men do for themselves, a "Parliament of Men". It is not something that men do even out of obedience to God, a "Congress of Religions". It is God's act in drawing man to Himself in Jesus Christ. In that act He uses the existence of His people among the nations, who, in so far as they are drawn into the Christ-event, are "a city set on a hill that cannot be hid", the "new Jerusalem" into which men come to worship. He uses that witness to the Christ-event to gather men from all nations to Himself. But it is not the witness, but God's use of it, which gathers His people into Christ. The Christian mission cannot create the new people of God: God uses it for His purpose of judgment and of gathering.

The Mission of Christ is thus the act of the Triune God. For Jesus Christ is sent forth into the world from God the Creator, the source and ground of all that is, for the fulfilment of His purpose in creation. In His obedience and self-giving He carries out that purpose and then "ascends" to God, offering to God His completed work. And in this "last hour" God the Holy Spirit, through the testimony of those who have been drawn into this total Event—incarnation, ministry, crucifixion, resurrection, ascension—brings

196

the final word of judgment and of new life to all men and gathers those who respond into the new humanity, to the praise of God through Jesus Christ, the new Temple, which is the consummation of His creation.

The sign of this consummation is the manifestation of the love of Christ amongst those who are drawn into the new humanity. This is the fruit of His risen life, and the token in this "last hour" of the life of the age to come. It is both a witness to the world of the character of its true life and a foretaste in this present age of the life of a new heaven and a new earth. The people of God in this historical era are the community of "the end" and they manifest the life of the end in their being bound together in love, whereby mankind may be brought to faith and so to the life which God designed for it.

The goal of the Mission of Christ, and therefore of those who participate in His Mission, is that a re-created humanity may adore His God and Father, which is the true end of man. In the last analysis, it is not an activity we engage in to save men from themselves: we engage in it because what God has done for men in Jesus Christ makes us delight to praise Him. It is not a harsh endeavour, heavy with gloom and grimness: it is a joyful hymn of adoration.

To share in Christ's Mission is to join the whole choir of heaven in the adoration of His Father and our Father, His God and our God. It is to share by faith in His ascension. It is to join in a doxology, sung by the first representatives of a new humanity, that all mankind may join in the praise of God which is the true meaning of its existence. The calling of men's creative activities to their true goal in Christ is the calling of them to die to self-sufficiency and surrender themselves to their true end, which is the praise of God. The offering of life in mission, giving it over to service or giving it up in testimony, is sharing in the surrendered life of Christ which is His glorification, His "doxology". The proclamation of the name of the Redeemer is an act of praise to God and thereby an invitation to men, by accepting that redemption, to join in that praise whose music is the hidden meaning of all things.

To share in Christ's Mission is to let the world overhear our praises. It is a liturgical act. The Lord's Supper is its prefiguring and the foretaste of its completion. The Lord's Supper brings the created world to the praise of God with the handiwork of men upon it—not wheat and grapes but bread and wine are the offering. It offers new life in Christ to those who die to themselves and are raised with Him. It binds them into one, not with the bonds of human goodwill, but by participation in His death and resurrection. It draws them here and now into the life of the age to come. It is done in thanksgiving, that in the Event of Jesus Christ, He who created the world is drawing all things to their end in Him. It is mission, for it articulates the Christ-event in the present age. It is gathering, for in it Christ gathers His people with their life in this world to their true centre. It is doxology, for in it God is praised and glorified.

Mission is nothing else than this—to speak, to act, to live so as to "cause his glory to be praised".[3] To share in Christ's Mission is to be joined with all the host of heaven in that doxology which is the final hymn of all the universe:

> "Unto him that sitteth upon the throne and unto the Lamb be the blessing and the honour and the glory and the dominion for ever and ever."

NOTES

1. Cp. e.g. Rom. 1–2.
2. Cp. Phil. 3: 20, Luke 11: 20.
3. Rev. 5, Matt. 25: 31–46.
4. John 1: 5, Rev. 21: 23–24.
5. Col. 3: 1–3, Matt. 28: 20*b*.
6. 2 Cor. 5: 17, Rom. 8: 22–25.
7. Eph. 2: 12.
8. Rom. 7: 23, Gal. 5: 1. In Johannine language it is a life in "darkness".
9. Rom. 1: 28 f.
10. 2 Cor. 1: 9, 1 John 3: 14.
11. Phil. 3: 12, Eph. 2: 8, Rom. 8: 24–25.
12. Rom. 12: 1, Eph. 1: 12.
13. Phil. 3: 12, cp. Col. 3. T. W. Manson: *Ethics and the Gospel* (London, 1960) points out (p. 51) that the Sermon on the Mount "is saying: 'This is how you who are in the Kingdom of God must live if your citizenship is to be a reality.'"
14. Rom. 10: 14 ff., 2 Cor. 5: 20.
15. "Truth" (*alētheia*) in the Fourth Gospel means eternal reality as revealed to men, and involves a personal union with Christ: see C. H. Dodd: *The Interpretation of the Fourth Gospel* (Cambridge 1953), pp. 170–78. "Eternal life" (*zoē aiōnios*) is the life of the age to come experienced here and now, and so life which is real life: cp. *ibid.*, pp. 144–50.
16. Gal. 4: 8, Rev. 2–3.
17. Rom. 6: 12 f., 8: 12 f.
18. John 3: 17, Acts 3: 26, 7: 35, 10: 36, 1 John 4: 9 f., Gal. 4: 4, Rom. 8: 3.
19. Col. 1: 13, 1 Pet. 1: 3, Rev. 1: 6.
20. The N.T. has many evidences of conflict with such Gnostic views. Cp. e.g. the emphatic affirmation of the historical nature of the event of Jesus Christ at the opening of 1 John.
21. See Col. 1 and Eph. 1.
22. Col. 1: 15, cp. John 1: 1–18, 2 Cor. 5: 19.
23. Matt. 16: 17, cp. 1 Cor. 12: 3.

Chapter 2

1. Phil. 2: 8.
2. Rom. 6: 3–4.
3. 1 Cor. 10: 16.
4. Cp. the Fourth Gospel's presentation of Jesus' offering of His life as an act which "glorifies" God: see e.g. John 12: 27 f. For His life as an act of service, see Mark 10 :45= Matt. 20: 28 and Luke 22: 27.
5. See Phil. 3: 12.
6. Acts 4: 12.

Chapter 3

1. The MS. of this book was completed before H. Richard Niebuhr: *Radical Monotheism and Western Culture* (London 1961) came into my hands. It is a powerful and penetrating treatment of the theme of this paragraph.
2. 1 Cor. 15: 20–28, Eph. 2: 13–16.
3. Cp. C. H. Dodd in *New Testament Studies* (1953), pp. 129 ff.: "In Christ man is confronted with the law of his creation." See also the remarks of M. M. Thomas: "Culture and Religion" (in *I.R.M.* April 1961, p. 208) on the need for a theology which will do justice to "what may be called the human ultimates" in the cultural renascence in Asia and provide a "criterion to distinguish between the human and inhuman in it". . . . "A devotion to the truly human in a real sense implies and expresses a partial but true response to God, and is at least the door at which the knocking of God-in-Christ is heard."
4. This paragraph touches on one aspect of the relationship between God's action in "secular" history and His action in redemption—a question with which ecumenical discussion of mission constantly finds itself confronted. It was one of the subjects noted by Norman Goodall as requiring further discussion after the Willingen Meeting of the I.M.C. (1952). He formulated it thus:

"What is the relation between 'history' and 'salvation history', between God's activity in creation and His grace in redemption? For many this question arises out of an urgent missionary concern to help men understand the world in which they live, the age in which they live, and the points at which, within the ordinary stuff of their existence and in a particular 'year of grace', they may trace the Hand and discern the Presence of the Redeemer." (Norman Goodall, Ed., *Missions under the Cross* (London 1953), pp. 20 f.)

It is significant that the Mexico Meeting of the C.W.M.E. encountered it afresh, in several different contexts. The Section on "The Witness of the Congregation to its Neighbourhood" expressed it thus:

"The discussion raised a theological issue which remained unresolved. Debate returned again and again to the relationship between God's action in and through the church and everything God is doing in the world apparently independently of the Christian community. Can a distinction be drawn between God's providential action and God's redeeming action? If the restoration and reconciliation of human life is being achieved by the action of God through secular agencies, what is the place and significance of faith? If the church is to be wholly involved in the world, and its history, what is the true nature of its separateness? We were able to state thesis and antithesis in this debate, but we could not see our way through to the truth we feel lies beyond this dialectic. Yet we believe that all attempts to adapt the structures or the thinking of the church to match the great changes that are taking place in the world will be doomed to paralysis until we can find the way through to a truer understanding of the relation between the world and the church in the purpose of God."

This is clearly one of the points at which those engaged in mission are raising an urgent issue with the theologians, and on which it would be reasonable to expect further work from the theologians. But it is possible that its recurrence in ecumenical discussion of mission, without apparently very much progress towards an agreed answer in the decade since Willingen, is an indication that the possibility of enlightenment and an agreed answer depends not only on theological study and discussion, but also on more and bolder experiments in practice to live in and by the saving act of God in Christ outside the bounds of the ecclesiastical sphere and in trust through that saving act in God's providential governance of the created world and its historical process.

The issue arises at later points in this present essay: see e.g. Chapter 4, especially pp. 52 ff., Chapter 5, especially pp. 61 ff., and Chapters 9 and 10.

5. Cp. the report of the Section at the Mexico Meeting on "The Witness of Christians to Men in the Secular World":

"Secular structures have a God-given function to serve men by bringing them into new relationships for production, or education, or the exercise of political power. Structures deny their purpose when they become self-serving or when they reduce men to objects or functions. New powers in the hands of men and vast organizations in which to exercise them open new opportunities both for service and for exploitation of men. Both are happening in our world. The fight for justice to individuals and minorities is not over, and Christians need to join with all who are prepared to engage in it."

1. Eph. 1: 9, 10, NEB.

2. Cp. Eph. 1: 9, NEB, "He has made known to us his *hidden* purpose" (*mysterion*).

3. Rom. 8: 19–25.

4. Gen. 1: 28, cp. Ps. 8: 5 f.

5. The meeting at Mexico had a good deal to say on this point. The report of the Section on "The Witness of Christians to Men in the Secular World" is largely concerned with it. While recognizing that "secularization opens up possibilities of new freedom and new enslavement for men", it insists that:

> "As Christians we are involved with all mankind in the process of secularization and with the making of these choices [*sc.* between greater freedom and new enslavement] which present themselves not once but again and again. . . . Christian witness participates in the common agony and hope which men experience in the process of secularization. It should articulate questions and answers from within the modern world and take up the points of decision which God Himself has provided through secularization. Thus we can come to a deeper understanding of the presence of Jesus Christ in the world and communicate the gospel."

6. Luke 13: 29, Matt. 8: 11.

7. Eph. 2: 14.

8. Rev. 21: 24–26.

9. Cp. Karl Barth: *An Exegetical Study of St. Matthew 28: 16–20* in Gerald H. Anderson (Ed.) *The Theology of the Christian Mission* (New York 1961), p. 64. N. A. Dahl: "The People of God", in the *Ecumenical Review*, Jan. 1957. E. Perry: *The Gospel in Dispute* (New York 1958), p. 34.

10. Gal. 4: 26.

11. 1 Pet. 2: 9 f.

12. Ps. 96: 5.

13. Mark 11: 17.

14. Cp. John 11: 51–52, Eph. 2: 11–22.

15. This seems the preferable interpretation of "the least of these my brethren", rather than taking that phrase to mean "Christians". See McNeile, *ad loc.*, and Jeremias: *The Parables of Jesus* (E. T. London 1954), p. 143.

16. Cp. Ethelbert Stauffer: *New Testament Theology* (E.T. London 1955), p. 195:

> "God pursues mankind, the whole of mankind, with the gospel of Christ. But the peoples of the world take offence at the gospel, all the peoples without exception! And even more than this: each people takes offence in its own peculiar way, and has its own

grounds for rejecting the word of the cross, its own reasons for
holding back. So each people must find its own specific way
through its peculiar hindrance. Every people says its own peculiar
'no' to Jesus Christ, crucifies Him afresh in its own way—and so
comes, by its own road, to that point of extinction where all self-
glory is at an end, and Jesus Christ is the *ultima ratio*. But it is along
this road that the inexhaustibility of the Gospel comes to light. For
the universality of the gospel finds its historical expression in the
fact that it has something specific to say to each particular people
and to its particular questions. So we can say about the operation
of the gospel among the various peoples of the world just what had
to be said about its operation in the various epochs of history. It
serves the same final purpose: the unfolding of the mystery of
Christ to the glory of God the Father (cp. Eph. 3: 8 ff., 16 ff.)."
See also Perry: *op. cit.*, p. 77.

Chapter 5

1. Speaking on "The World in which we preach Christ" at the
opening of the Mexico Meeting, M. M. Thomas, of the Christian Institute for the Study of Religion and Society, Bangalore, drew attention to the fact that science and technology had made men less directly
and constantly dependent on "raw nature" and had made possible the
creation of a "second nature" which does man's bidding. One implication of this is "a heightened sense of human creativity. In one
sense, the many revolts against religion in the past two or three centuries have all been to release man's creativity, which was suppressed
by religion and the dictates of religious authority. The relation of the
gospel to human creativity is still to be thought out." Here is another
question arising from mission for the theologians.

2. The report of the Section at the Mexico Meeting on "The Witness of the Congregation in its Neighbourhood" includes the following:

"Because we are the pilgrim people of God moving on towards
the new heaven and new earth and seeking both to be and to point
to the signs of Christ's redeeming purpose for His whole creation, it
is of the nature of the Church to be open to those new forms of
church life needed for our witness to the Lordship of Christ within
the changing forms of life. . . . We would suggest some of the types
of form needed to-day.

"(*a*) 'Cell' groups (perhaps becoming new forms of congregation)
meeting in the particular 'neighbourhoods' (sociological
communities) such as residential communities, trade unions,.

political life, business. Only in this way can men hear the Word and experience the fellowship of Christ at the places where their anxieties and hopes are faced and where their important decisions are made. Theological reflection must take place at the points where obedience is required.

"(*b*) Congregational forms that transcend these particular realms of social life and witness to the power of Christ to bring forth a new humanity which breaks through the separation of class, culture, concern that so often characterize the separate 'neighbourhoods'. So, for example, a congregation based in a segregated suburb in New Jersey (USA), where all the residents are white middle class is called to find a form of congregational life that breaks through the separations of race, class and culture.

"(*c*) Forms of church life which reach out into the vital streams of contemporary life where the fabric of human existence is being woven. Thus, in Latin America the church is being called to find forms which will enable it to witness to Christ's purpose in the midst of the incredible awakening of the masses to the task of demolition of an evil social order—an awakening that constitutes a marvellous conversion from fatalism to hope, from indolence to revolutionary action and from resignation to rebellion. Again the church is called to find the forms which will enable the laity to be trained to witness to Christ as they go to other lands for government, or industry, or education and play their part in the emergence of the new world community. These two examples point to the importance of the truths we are beginning to rediscover—that the church is to equip its people to be God's servants in the world, and that new forms of congregational life are needed for the fulfilment of this calling."

3. Cp. the report of the Section of the Mexico Meeting on "The Witness of the Christian Church across National and Confessional Boundaries":

"It is not enough merely to cross frontiers physically. God's mission demands total involvement in the life of the church beyond the frontier, as members of the one Body. Every such involvement is a source of joy for those who are ready to bear the pain of estrangement. In the providence of God the very handicaps and frustrations of foreignness may be for the furtherance of the Gospel and part of the 'Wisdom of God' (1 Cor. 2: 7). For every Christian is an 'alien' in this world, while in the household of faith there are 'no more strangers and foreigners'."

Chapter 6

1. Cp. the "Statement" received by the Ghana Assembly of the I.M.C. (1957–58):

"The Christian world mission is Christ's, not ours. Prior to all our efforts and activities, prior to all our gifts of service and devotion, God sent His Son into the world. And He came in the form of a servant—a servant who suffered even to the death of the Cross. . . . We believe it is urgent that this word of judgment and mercy should be given full freedom to cleanse and redeem our present activities, lest our human pride in our activities hinder the free course of God's mission in the world." (Ronald K. Orchard, Ed.: *The Ghana Assembly of the I.M.C.*, 1957–58 (London 1958, p. 180.)

2. See J. Jeremias: *Jesus' Promise to the Nations* (E.T. London 1958) and J. Blauw: *The Missionary Nature of the Church* (London 1962), pp. 83 ff.

Chapter 7

1. Reinhold Niebuhr: *The Godly and the Ungodly* (London 1959), p. 142.

2. Cp. Col. 1: 16 ff., Rom. 11: 36, 1 Cor. 8: 6, 2 Cor. 5: 17.

3. Cp. the remark of the Section at the Mexico Meeting on "The Witness of Christians to Men of Other Faiths", speaking of "the nature of dialogue":

"Whatever the circumstances may be, our intention in every human dialogue should be to be involved in the dialogue of God with men, and to move our partner and ourself to listen to what God in Christ reveals to us, and to answer Him."

4. 2 Cor. 4: 5 f., NEB. I owe the thought in this paragraph to a Bible Study led by Erik W. Nielsen.

5. 2 Cor. 4: 10–12, NEB.

6. Cp. the report of the Section at the Mexico Meeting on "The Witness of Christians to Men of Other Faiths":

"The Christian's fundamental approach to a man of another faith must be the recognition that, for him, Christ has already broken down every barrier. He meets his fellow man as a brother for whom Christ has already died. He will welcome every common interest and every common concern through which he can enter into real fellowship, living his life as a concerned participant in the community of which he is a part."

7. Cp. Matt. 19: 16–20=Mark 10: 17–31=Luke 18: 18–30.

8. M. A. C. Warren in the *CMS Newsletter*, No. 209, Oct. 1958.

Chapter 8

1. The meeting of the C.W.M.E. at Mexico is one sign of this, as may be seen from its composition, the structure of its programme, and its findings. Cp. the conclusion of its "Message" quoted in the Preface.

2. Gal. 2: 20, NEB.

Chapter 9

1. See C. N. Cochrane: *Christianity and Classical Culture* (New York 1957: first edition 1940), pp. 221 f.

2. Trans. by E. J. Goodspeed in *The Apostolic Fathers* (New York 1950).

3. See T. M. Parker: *Christianity and the State in the Light of History* (London 1955), pp. 35–42.

4. The provisions of the Edict of Milan, March 313, are the following:

(From Lactantius, *De Mort. Pers.* c. xlviii.)

"2. When we, Constantine and Licinius, emperors, had an interview at Milan, and conferred together with respect to the good and security of the commonweal, it seemed to us that, amongst those things that are profitable to mankind in general, the reverence paid to the Divinity merited our first and chief attention, and that it was proper that the Christians and all others should have liberty to follow that mode of religion which to each of them appeared best; so that that God who is seated in heaven, might be benign and propitious to us, and to every one under our government.

"3. And therefore we judged it a salutary measure, and one highly consonant to right reason, that no man should be denied leave of attaching himself to the rites of the Christians, or to whatever other religion his mind directed him, that thus the supreme Divinity, to whose worship we freely devote ourselves, might continue to vouchsafe his favour and beneficence to us.

"4. And accordingly we give you to know that, without regard to any provisos in our former orders to you concerning the Christians, all who choose that religion are to be permitted, freely and absolutely, to remain in it, and not to be disturbed any way, or molested.

"5. And we thought fit to be thus special in the things committed to your charge, that you might understand that the indulgence which we have granted in matters of religion to the Christians is ample and unconditional.

"6. And perceive at the same time that the open and free exercise of their respective religions is granted to all others, as well as to the Christians; for it befits the well-ordered state, and the tranquillity of our times, that each individual be allowed, according to his own choice, to worship the Divinity; and we mean not to derogate aught from the honour due to any religion or its votaries.

"7. Moreover with respect to the Christians, we formerly gave certain orders concerning the places appropriated for their religious assemblies; but now we will that all persons who have purchased such places, either from our exchequer or from any one else, do restore them to the Christians, without money demanded or price claimed, and that this be performed peremptorily and unambiguously."

(Clauses 8 and 9 provide that church buildings received by gift and any other places belonging to Christians are to be restored to them. Owners may apply for compensation. Clauses 10, 11 and 12 enjoin diligence in seeing that the orders are obeyed so that divine favour may continue, and require the Ordinance to be published.)

Translation as given in B. J. Kidd (Ed.): *Documents illustrative of the History of the Church,* Vol. 1 (London 1920), pp. 234–35. The Latin text, with a different English translation, is given in H. M. Gwatkin: *Selections from Early Writers illustrative of Church History to the time of Constantine* (London 1914: first edition 1893), pp. 170–75. A third English translation of most of the Edict appears in H. Bettenson (Ed.): *Documents of the Christian Church* (London 1943), pp. 22–23.

5. Cochrane, *op. cit.,* p. 179.

6. Cp. Cochrane, *op. cit.,* p. 217.

7. The following paragraphs refer only to non-Roman Catholic missions. I am not competent to discuss the development of Roman Catholic mission theory and practice in this connection.

8. M. M. Thomas, speaking to the Mexico Meeting on "The World in which we preach Christ", said:

"The structures of Christendom broke down long ago, but even Protestant Missions continued to conceive Christendom as an ideology, and in fact the Mission Compounds of Asia and Africa were set up as little Christendoms—societies under Christian control. This was in part inevitable because non-Christian communities too were religious-doms and therefore change of religion meant ostracism from traditional communities."

Chapter 10

1. Arend Th. van Leeuwen: *Christianity in World History: The Meeting of the Faiths of East and West* (London, 1964) appeared while

this book was in the press. This thorough and comprehensive study has much to say of relevance to the themes of the present essay and particularly to this chapter, e.g. p. 408 f.

2. The horizontal process of transmission of a culture may also be questioned on other bases than an explicit loyalty to Jesus Christ—for example, on grounds of loyalty to truth or goodness, and this is related to God's providential ordering of the world. But we are here concerned with an educational system claiming to be explicitly Christian, and therefore with the relation of the process of transmission to the Christ-event.

3. Cp. e.g. 1 John 3: 13, 1 Pet. 4: 12.

4. Cp. W. A. Visser 't Hooft, in an address to the Mexico Meeting on "Missions as the Test of Faith":

"The missionary witness is at all times a test of the faith of the Church. But there are times when the testing process is more or less hidden (we might speak of underground testing). And there are other times when the testing is very much above ground and demonstrably acute. The normal situation is rather the situation of open conflict. Must we not look on the period from roughly the middle of the nineteenth to the middle of the twentieth century as a sort of armistice period in the relation between missions and the world? The contradiction of the world was more or less *sotto voce* and there was sufficient outside encouragement so as not to notice these negative voices. The encouragement which came from the world and sometimes even from the Church was often given for the wrong reasons. Somehow missions seemed to become an accepted part of modern civilization."

He went on to point out that we are now entering a period of testing:

"Many more churches have become churches under pressure. The numbers of non-Christians living outside the reach of any form of organized evangelistic and missionary action have vastly increased. And the so-called Christian countries are more and more becoming *pays de mission*. Other great world religions have become mission-minded and enter, not without success, the traditionally Christian territories. At the same time the right of the Church to be a missionary church is challenged in all parts of the world."

5. In his speech at the Mexico Meeting to which reference has already been made, M. M. Thomas called attention to the fact that:

"Men, whether secular or religious, are asking questions to-day to which the Gospel is challengingly relevant. . . . The significance of modern secularism and modern renaissance of ancient religions is precisely that for the first time they are in a situation in which

Chapter 10

Christianity can participate because the questions which they are asking about human existence and salvation are those for which the Gospel has the answer. Men, whether secular or religious, are concerned with freedom, its responsibilities and anxieties, its purpose and tragedy, so that questions about the meaning of existence including the problem of sin, law and grace, guilt and salvation, alienation and reconciliation and the relation between justice and love are raised existentially. It is only as the Christian Missions are patterned to participate in the common agony of articulating those questions and answers to them within the framework of contemporary life and language that they can understand in depth the meaning of Jesus Christ for to-day and communicate the Gospel of His Salvation to others."

6. Col. 1: 13 RSV.
7. *Ibid.*, 1: 12.

Chapter 11

1. Gen. 28: 14 RSV.
2. John 11: 52.
3. 1 Cor. 15: 20 f., Jas. 1: 18, Rev. 14: 4.

Chapter 12

1. This is a consequence, and not a contradiction, of what was said earlier (p. 69), about "foreign" mission being the essential form of mission.

2. The Mexico Meeting had much to say about the dispersion of Christians into "secular" life as part of mission, but it did not consider the question of the relation of missionaries as such to that dispersion, nor the question of the responsibility of organizations for mission in regard to it.

Chapter 13

1. Mark 7: 13.
2. 1 Pet. 2: 9.
3. Rev. 5: 12.

Conclusion

1. This para. is based on J. Jeremias: *Jesus' Promise to the Nations* (E.T. London 1958), pp. 57 ff.
2. On Matt. 28: 18–20 as a "coronation hymn" see J. Jeremias: *op. cit.*, p. 38 f., and J. Blauw: *op. cit.*, p. 83, quoting O. Michel.
3. See Eph. 1: 11–14 NEB:

"In Christ indeed we have been given our share in the heritage, as was decreed in his design whose purpose is everywhere at work. For it was his will that we, who were the first to set our hope on Christ, should *cause his glory to be praised*. And you too, when you had heard the message of the truth, the good news of your salvation, and had believed it, became incorporate in Christ and received the seal of the promised Holy Spirit: and that Spirit is the pledge that we shall enter upon our heritage, when God has redeemed what is his own, to his praise and glory."

INDEX

AFRICA, 122
Anabaptists, 117
Anderson, Gerald H., 202
Anglicans, 118
Asia, 56

BARTH, Karl, 202
Bechuanaland, 119
Bettenson, H., 207
Blauw, J. C., 205, 209

CALVIN, 117
Ceylon, 118
Christendom, 53–6, 60, 69, 97–100, 115–120, 153, 177–178, 181, 207
Cochrane, C. N., 206, 207
Commission on World Mission & Evangelism, 6, 7, 8, 200, 206
Congregationalists, 119
Constantine, 111, 206
Cunliffe-Jones, H., 7

DAHL, N. A., 202
Dodd, C. H., 199, 200

Ecumenical Review, 202
Evangelical Revival, 119

FIFTH Monarchy Men, 117

GHANA, 205
Gnostic, 199
Goodall, Norman, 200
Goodspeed, E. J., 206
Gwatkin, H. M., 207

HAYWARD, Victor, 7
Holy Roman Empire, 117

INTERNATIONAL Missionary Council, 7, 8, 200, 205
International Review of Missions, 200
Israel, 22, 26, 55, 56, 195
Israel, State of, 56

JEREMIAS, J., 202, 205, 209
Judaism, 56
Justin, 111

KIDD, B. J., 207

LACTANTIUS, 206
Licinius, 206
Luther, Martin, 117

MANSON, T. W., 199
McNeile, 202
Mexico City, 6, 8, 9, 200–209
Michel, O., 209